# SEX INCORPORATED

A POSITIVE VIEW OF THE SEXUAL REVOLUTION

by Hans F. Hofmann

BEACON PRESS                    BOSTON

# ACKNOWLEDGMENTS

WHEN the first draft of this essay was being written Claude A. Smith, Ph.D., was my colleague and research associate in the Institute for Human Development, Inc. Our discussions were significant in the formulation of this study. While Dr. Smith is in no way responsible for any errors or shortcomings in the manuscript, he did generously contribute in several ways to the study; and his assistance deserves mention to the reader.

# CONTENTS

# SEX INCORPORATED

A POSITIVE VIEW OF THE SEXUAL REVOLUTION

# CHAPTER I

# SEX INCORPORATED

WHAT IS DIFFERENT about sex today from the way it was fifty years ago? The most striking difference is that sex has become an extremely familiar public characteristic of our modern way of life. We encounter sexual references all around us in such profusion that we hardly recognize any more how an all-permeating sexual flavor dominates our sense of life.

Sex has ceased to be just the private activity of married men and women necessary for the procreation of their children. Sex has come to be accepted and exploited in a variety of ways which, on the surface, seem to have little in common. Not only is sex an activity; it is also a commodity, a symbol of emancipation, a key ingredient in advertising, and the most enduring of the modern "kicks." It is welcome social progress that sex has been liberated from the stuffy confines of the Victorian bedroom. But we are still far from being able to understand all the nuances of *sex* as the relationship of two persons, and of *sexuality* as an awareness that we are sexual creatures, able to express ourselves through our bodies.

The advertising and entertainment industries capitalize on the delight we take in being—or at least watching—attractive young persons with well-shaped bodies. An automobile advertisement may utilize most of its space presenting elegantly dressed, beautiful people in front of a mansion, ready to embark for a festive evening in the car in question. Little is said about the technical qualities of the car. Nor is there any consideration of how well the human models really know how to live.

One need not be so naïve as to believe that in the advertising agency's view a desire to be like the models is going to make us rush out and buy a car. On the contrary, the urbane people are there to draw our attention to the joy of possessing and using the advertised product. The elegance and sexiness of the models rub off on the image of the car itself, so that the car seems appetizing in its photographed setting.

It is, of course, possible to mistake the message of the advertisement. We may feel subtly judged and found wanting by the glamour depicted in the prestige ad. Turning against ourselves, we may ask why we cannot afford to live like this. If we imagine that pleasure is best insured by luxurious surroundings, we may simply accuse ourselves of not making enough money. It is not necessarily true that the fancy gadgets and luxurious extras have been sexually oversold. The fault may well lie with us. We have underestimated our personal and interpersonal ability and responsibility to enrich our lives through our inner resources. Surroundings will not do that for us.

The crucial issue, therefore, is whether or not we are able and confident to respond selectively to what all around us is suggested as the real fun of living. If we run from one suggestion and promise to the next, always trusting that the new thing offered will heighten our enjoyment of life, we shall fill our shopping bag while emptying out any inner confidence that we can be creators and masters of our own lives. Constant references to sex in advertising, movies, television, the theater, and books do not constitute our dilemma. These media of communication merely point out that sex is everywhere around us. Banning sex from mass media would be futile as well as impossible; the message has already gotten across that life is sexual and that we have to learn to live as sexual beings.

The proper question is not how and when to censor what appears daily, but how to respond. If what is presented is distorted, exhibitionistic, and repulsive, we are free to turn away.

Social responsibility rests directly on us to exercise good judgment. The mass media and their sponsors are far too sensitive to commercial success to keep foisting on us what we have clearly decided not to buy. It is our inner attitude which determines how vulnerable we are to external pressure. In the face of intense bombardment of sexually flavored sales appeals one need not yield to the proposition that happiness is bought in the supermarket or taught on the movie screen. Sexuality itself can offer us a key to discovering and defining our own strengths and resources. It moves us toward others in ways that reveal how experience can broaden and change our awareness and enjoyment of life.

## WHAT IS SEXUALITY?

That sexuality itself actually pushes us toward greater self-awareness is an uncommon viewpoint. In the past sexuality has usually been treated as an aspect of the personality separate from and inferior to the rational ego. Moreover, human sexuality has often been described as an eruptive and disruptive force controllable only through the rational intervention of personal restraint and social rules or laws. Marriage, for instance, was supposed to domesticate the wildness of sexual impulses and guide them into the peaceful course of childbearing.

Even Freud was convinced that social controls were necessary to prevent men from giving free rein to sexual desires at the expense of social order. Sexuality, identified closely and exclusively with the instinctual urge, appeared to be a potentially chaotic force which even the most reasonable of men could barely master. No respectable man in his right mind would link too closely his personal self-esteem or his social reputation with that dangerous explosive, his sexuality. We still habitually discuss sexuality as something a man "has" rather than something he "is." We are likely to speak of sexuality in the same detached way that we speak of having sexual organs as part of the human anatomy.

To begin with the widest possible circumscription, sexuality encompasses a manifold awareness of being incomplete. On the several levels of personality—the instinctual, the emotional, the conscious, and the unconscious—sexuality urges us to seek what will make us complete. The instinctual factor contributes a glandular motor drive to sexuality. Even the instinctual needs for sleep, food, and shelter include the emotional, artistic aspects of dream-awareness, refined taste, and aesthetic judgment; and sexuality we judge to be a more complicated drive than these other and simpler instincts. Sexuality, however, comprises far more than the merely instinctual.

Sexuality is complicated in part by its indispensable involvement with another person. The unconscious mind generates vivid and specific fantasies of how sexual urges could be satisfied. But these fantasies entail a partner who embodies the qualities to which we sexually respond, a partner who enlivens our fantastic sexual enjoyment through erotic cooperation. The rational, conscious mind weighs those qualifications which we expect in a partner in order to assure successful living together. In anticipatory thought or imagination we appraise the pros and cons of constant and lasting living together with a specific person.

Knowledge of the diverse components in human sexuality should not lead to any inference that sexual development is a simple, neat process. Nor is sexual development inevitably haphazard. Crystallizing and strengthening one's identity demands that several aspects of sexuality be intertwined and thereby refined. It is as impossible to conceive of an unsexual human personality as it is to understand sexuality without seeing it as an integral and decisive part of the whole personality, and thus central in one's attempt to develop an integrated, wholesome personality. The Freudian theory of libido as the prime life-force cannot be maintained without serious amendments which are bound to expand our understanding of the concept. But Freud is right: sexuality constitutes the red thread along which we discern the problems and the promise of personal growth. Human development cannot be measured or characterized without relying on sexual growth as its prime indicator.

No man is an island to himself. If an understanding of man depends exclusively upon introspective scrutiny of one's moods and changes, it is as lopsided as the understanding which only counts people as numbers on a statistical scale. Sexuality explodes the dangerous illusion of any such one-sidedness by being at once the most personal and intensively interpersonal human experience. Who one is can be determined only by interaction between the self and others.

Sexuality forces each person to assess his personal identity by appraising how able he is to share himself with others without losing his sense of independence. The sexual move toward another reveals both inner hopes and fears. Indeed, sexuality does not relent until a human has dealt with his ability to be intimately at case with another human.

In view of the power and pervasiveness of sexuality, it is not surprising that men try to establish external, popularly accepted and supported moral structures to govern sexual behavior. The less we accept and trust ourselves, the smaller our confidence in others' ability to behave themselves. Hence we call for a public authority, church, or school to establish binding rules that surround sex with a restrictive safety belt. But in a pluralistic society it is increasingly difficult to ascertain a clear social consensus about the nature and potentialities of sexuality. Not only parents and their youngsters, but parents-among-themselves and young-people-among-their-peers differ widely as to how dangerous sexual liberty is and how sexual responsibility should be fostered.

The diversity of personal opinions and the vacuum resulting from the erosion of religious and other social authorities over sexuality demand the personal recognition that one is shouldering a vaster responsibility than ever before for self-understanding, growth, and behavior. In a democratic society, based on the religious ideal of man as the executor of God's will, we should no longer shy away from growing up to take responsibility for our own attitudes and actions.

Part of the new burden of personal responsibility is eased by our knowing something about the character of sexuality. Clinical studies and social surveys have widened our intellectual grasp of sexual development. Sexuality, nevertheless, harbors at its center a profound ambivalence that more knowledge cannot dissolve. There remains an inescapable struggle between self-indulgence and self-criticism, between high idealism and positive self-acceptance, between seeking fusion with the other and withdrawing to safer isolation, between relying on external authority and asserting personal independence. This ambivalence, although by no means exclusively their problem, is most striking among adolescents.

Sexuality is for the young a symbol of emancipation from family control and a foretaste of important, independent actions to come. Young people's expectations about the creativity of sexuality are generally high and their criticisms of the failures of their elders are disarmingly perceptive. Yet they are already learning that sexuality plays the same somewhat mundane but significant role in their choices of partners and careers that it played for all generations before them. As our ancestors sometimes self-consciously "married into" holdings of power and land, so young people still marry into industrial corporations and social prominence.

We think easily of the adolescent as living on the borderline between two phases of development, childhood and maturity. The larger truth is that sexual man always lives on the borderline between finding and losing himself. He can never forget his strivings to be individual, nor can he escape being a particle in the social network of sexuality. The question is whether he can learn in time to live courageously on this borderline, not only accepting its inescapability but maturing by answering its challenge to unfold his inner resources.

What must be emphasized is the close and decisive connection between self-understanding and sexuality. A person must bring together—must incorporate into a unity—what he knows or thinks of himself with his condition as a sexual creature. Otherwise, and his high ideals notwithstanding, he is forever in danger of being overwhelmed by an ignored and uncultivated sexual impulse. Man does not live by sex alone; neither can he live by ignoring its challenge.

## WHAT IS SEX?

Sex is the action through which we accomplish what sexuality prompts us to do. The term *sex* should be rescued from its promiscuous meanings in common usage. Restored to its precise significance, sex connotes the interaction by which persons express their most intimate union. *Expression* is here the most crucial term. The intimacy and mutuality of two people's relationship with each other is not limited to or by sex. But sex expresses most intensely the character of such a union, for better or for worse. That is why sexual intercourse represents the quintessence of sex. From this center, sex radiates in a descending line of significance into all other forms of human interaction and intercourse.

For many of us, the first full recognition that as human beings we actually originated from sexual intercourse is a startling discovery. Adolescents speculate and fantasize about sex with their peer friends and idols in mind. But to picture their sedate parents engaged in such a naked, baffling action goes against the grain of good, obedient children. Nothing could better symbolize the haphazard, modest beginnings of human life than tracing its origin to sexual intercourse. Not soberly respectful forethought and planning on the part of our parents gives us life, but the instinctually and emotionally charged mingling of two bodies. Immediately one is tempted to ask whether a life with such humble beginning is worthwhile. Indeed, a life which never rises above the physical aspect of man has little value. By the same token, a life that cannot take seriously the reality and significance of the physical is not truly lived at all.

The broader and deeper meaning of sex is indicated by the change it brings about in those who maintain a serious sexual relationship. Out of the exclusiveness of two people living in marriage arise the children who break the exclusiveness into a family of three or more. There is an old saying that the first children of a marriage are the husband and wife who have learned to live together well enough to provide a home for their children. Nothing, as a matter of fact, seems to convey the creativity of sex better than its power to re-create the husband and wife as a "marriage" before they bear children.

In our time we sense more and more the profound importance of intimate living together as sex expresses it. Since the embracing and controlling structure of the rural family and community, consisting of many interdependent and related people, has given way to the independence of the nuclear family (husband, wife, and children) in the impersonal society of city and suburb, families are more on their own and far more exposed to the multiplicity of a wide-open and highly diversified society. Small wonder that the meaning of sex should have changed accordingly.

To the modernist, Victorian sex seems in retrospect to have been guilt ridden and inhibited. To the traditionalist, sex seems to have become mere gamesmanship, played with accent on diversion and distraction. Neither caricature is accurate; neither captures the essence of a changing attitude toward sex. Actually, when we listen to children talk about sex we hear a curious mixture of exultation and indifference. On the one hand, the mutual discovery of a shared life of their own elates the young, who might have assumed, from observing their elders, that life amounts to little more than drudgery or resented compromise and sacrifice. On the other hand, the same young people could often not care less about the religious, social, and ethnic customs and taboos which heretofore have sanctioned and safeguarded the traditional meaning of sex.

What has changed is our attitude toward the human body and our ability to learn from physical nature how to structure our living together. We are becoming more aware of and more relaxed about being made of flesh. We no longer "have" a body; we "are" a body. The things we design and manufacture reflect the shapes of our bodies and their parts. The more we delight in our physical bodies, the more we mold tools for living in the likeness of the human figure and limbs as if such tools were playful extensions of our bodies.

The regulative principles with which traditional religion and society sought to uphold the sanctity and dignity of sex produce confusion because they not only are rooted in ignorance about physical nature but run contrary to learning to live realistically with the body. Especially in the area of sex, current pronounced and maybe even underlying values and ideals often seem to have little actual effect on casual behavior. What is professed as proper and right often proves not at all helpful in dealing with a specific situation. The result is a conflict between momentary reaction and subsequent unease. In moments of confusion and distress we cope blindly with the predicament and are likely to follow the most immediate inclination and desire. Under the instinctual and emotional pressure of a sexually charged circumstance, we often enough throw moral considerations to the wind and function as an instinctual urge demands and emotions suggest. Once the immediate heat of sexual excitement has subsided, moral remorse and emotional self-rejection are all the more intense.

It may well be that an inability to bring together what we think we ought to be, feel, think, and do with what a physical nature actually allows and demands leads to the sexual disappointment and loss of interest in sex among many middle-aged couples. The wear and tear of family routine and obligations diminish the physical strength and freedom to re-create the sexual vitality and ecstasy of former days when love play and intercourse still held the fascination of being a new and absorbing experience. At the same time, all the memories of unresolved moral scruples and moments of guilt and self-rejection poison the eagerness and delight of seeking the other's sexual company; such inhibition may become especially strong when a parent believes that he or she must be a shining example for the children so that they, at least, will not bring upon themselves the same turmoil and inner conflict the adult still has not overcome.

But neither the young person's helpless bobbing at the mercy of instant ecstasy and lingering self-accusation nor his parents' abstention from sex is necessary. These can be avoided if one faces himself for who he is, understands himself realistically, and penetrates through both the alluring mask of seductive illusion and the sterile demeanor of moralistic idealism. A better understanding of sex becomes helpful only when it is honestly shared by the whole society. Otherwise, the realist becomes the persecuted martyr of social prudery and hypocrisy, which, in turn, discourages and prevents his living in the flesh without undue glitter or remorse.

What is actually the relationship between sex and the body? We "use" our bodies for many kinds of work and leisure, but in sex we do not use the body, we "express" it. Instincts, feelings, fantasies, and thoughts are welded into a total bodily expression which is all the more satisfactory the less it is self-conscious. Sex can never be successfully abstracted from earthy enjoyment of the fleshly nature of man.

Art and literature can often be recognized on the basis of their willingness or reluctance to accept the human body directly and comfortably. Some of the most heatedly erotic writing shies away from overt praise of human anatomy in favor of unrealistic but more suggestive fantasies. Greek and Renaissance art, however, presented the glory of man's body unabashedly without intimating any erotic guile or unadmitted lust. Our time is beginning to recapture the same spirit. Lacking yet the Greek or Renaissance freedom of unself-consciously admiring bodily beauty, our literature aims at such innocent joy by first underscoring that sexual ease with the body cannot be gained before sexuality is incorporated into one's self-awareness and self-acceptance.

If our society is actually experiencing a sexual crisis and not just perennial anxieties blown out of proper perspective, the crisis has to do with the quality, not the quantity, of sex. Our problem is not whether to have more sex or less; hence it cannot be resolved on the superficial level of dos and don'ts or the familiar arguments of decorum versus laxity. What way of life would be most congenial to our understanding of the potentials inherent in sex? Can we bring such a way of life into existence? These are the questions before us.

Obviously an appreciation of the significance of sex is complicated in large part because sex is a corporate endeavor. Whatever meaning and satisfaction it has for one partner must become evident and acceptable to the other. Therein lies the inescapable difficulty of two different people becoming one flesh. Widespread marital problems and a persistently high divorce rate demonstrate the extent to which corporate sexual life overtaxes resources. The symptoms of stress should not be attributed solely to the weaknesses of individuals or partners. Society itself plays a part in sexual triumphs and failures—something we do not always either understand or concede. Even when society's contribution to the sexual life of its members is acknowledged, the acknowledgment may be twisted into a handy scapegoat so that all difficulties are blamed on environmental circumstances. This merely compounds misunderstanding by positing an artificial split between individual desires and social restrictions.

The very nature of sex is instructive at this point. The mandatory nakedness and physical interdependence in intercourse make it impossible to detain the partner by stubbornly holding on to the fig leaf of social prudery. Sex is neither an individual right nor a social monopoly. Living together in marriage frees both partners to achieve pleasure and understanding that cannot be acquired alone. Society has a vested interest in the procreation of children: it must renew itself. Sex thus permits the society's instinct for self-preservation as well as self-renewal by meeting its members' personal, individual needs in a vital exchange for a social good that does not necessarily enslave anyone.

Critics of our society argue that we tend to develop unhealthy conflicts between special interest groups, and between "the individual" and "the society." The picket line and the unqualified grievance get chosen in preference to flexible negotiation, and slogans replace open discussion. In the face of social programs for voluntary self-help or voluntary philanthropic projects, many people retreat into anonymous privacy, preferring things as they are, wishing only to be spared direct threats or hurts. Sex is by no means exempt from being afflicted with the symptoms of such "opting out" of participation in the shaping of our corporate way of life. Some of the most poignant magazine cartoons keep us aware of the miseries of the downtrodden wife and the harassed husband, unable to enjoy each other's company or to question their way of life, unable to make any sense of it all—and certainly too exhausted to enjoy sex.

## INCORPORATING SEX

When sex turns stale we often turn either to sex manuals for new techniques or to erotic stimulation from popular magazines or other media. Perhaps there is a new and exciting suggestion we had overlooked, but which could restore our flagging zeal for sex. The art of loving, like any other art, does flourish under constant, concerned attention. Acquiring new ideas and insights is part of an unending attempt to enliven and enrich sexual exchange and satisfaction. None can claim to be such a perfect lover that there is no room for learning.

Since sex, however, is far more than a skillful technique, executed with self-conscious bravado, no manual, magazine, or magician can fill in for a more basic deficiency. Sex is an unwavering indicator of personal confidence and resourcefulness. A manual can only prescribe the finishing touch to physical performance. Sex is bound to suffer if, preoccupied with finesse, we are inhibited and cannot give ourselves unreservedly to the sex partner. The last thing needed in this case is any further heightening of anxiety about how we compare technically with the most experienced and suave lovers. The majority of us harbor enough feelings of inferiority about our appearance and technique, especially after we have watched the movies.

The thesis of this book proposes just the opposite. Incorporating sex into a way of life means removing obstacles to being natural and at ease. Setting high goals of sexual prowess only adds another burden to already encumbered lives. Another trick, another position, is not the way to incorporate sex. The real challenge consists in being so true to oneself that sharing oneself nakedly with another person will be unself-conscious and honest, not marred by exaggerated expectations or apprehensions based on past disappointments or unfulfilled fantasies.

Some may contend that it is better to let sex, and life in general, run its inevitable course than to interfere with high ambitions for the quality of sex or life. There is a vast gulf between indifference and noninterference. We argue here not for artificial interference with the natural unfolding of sex life, but for the removal of what could interfere. Avoiding the pitfalls of concentrating on sex techniques does not imply that "incorporation" is a passive attitude toward an inevitable development. On the contrary, it is a collecting of self, a husbanding of resources, a general stocktaking, and a greater immediacy between the partners. The body itself gives a clue to the character of incorporation. The limbs and organs can function only on the basis of integrated cooperation. As sexual beings we are bound to be unsatisfied unless we can actively build a unity of experience. Our society seems to have few confident people who shape for themselves a deeply satisfying common life.

Narcissism is a good example of an attitude which resists the incorporation of sex. Self-centeredness, fixation on one's own attractiveness, paired with undue concern for the conservation of one's youthful beauty—these are the psychological ingredients of narcissism. The term stems from a Greek myth about a handsome young man who falls in love with his own reflection in a pool. Leaning over to study every detail of his image, he loses his balance and drowns. The lure of his own appearance is too great and Narcissus, in order to be closer to what he means to himself, loses his life.

Oscar Wilde in *The Picture of Dorian Gray* masterfully refined the Greek tale by analyzing the inner uncertainty of a man who depends on the adoration of others for his self-esteem since he has no inner resources that allow him to develop independent self-confidence. He is bound to drown in the crowd, where he seeks in vain to find what he misses within himself. Miraculously, Dorian retains his youthful good looks while a portrait of him, painted at the height of his beauty, gradually shows the signs of decay in a shallow playboy who cannot face himself.

Narcissus is bent on reaffirming his beauty because he rightly does not trust it as the base for realistic self-appraisal or self-acceptance. The real base is not beauty but confidence—confidence that allows us to see and accept all of ourselves, even our ugly side and unattractive characteristics. True self-acceptance can never be conditional or selective. It cannot affirm what we like in our personality while stopping short of recognizing, or owning up to, the dark aspects.

Neither secret love of the self nor exhibitionism for the delight and approval of others yields incorporation. The irony of these substitutes is explicitly clear in the Playboy Clubs. The Bunnies suggest a kind of narcissism in their frank calling of attention to carefully displayed physical attributes. The rules of the club, however, make quite clear that Bunnies are to be seen but not touched. The juxtaposition of being deliberately alluring but equally deliberately withdrawn defines strikingly the opposite of what we are aiming at in this book.

Each of the alternatives to incorporated sex makes sex a goal and an object. But we cannot integrate personhood *into* sex because sex is not a goal in itself. Sex expresses, and therefore verifies, personhood but does not actually establish it. On the contrary, we must sincerely and actively incorporate sex into our whole life as we become growingly aware of it in many ways and throughout different phases and ages.

Popular conceptions still assume that sex is acquired in adolescence and given up in late middle age, that it has its time and place but should not interfere with serious actions and obligations. It would be more helpful to acknowledge that we are conceived in sexual cohabitation and born as sexual beings. The beginning of puberty signals the triggering of emotional and physiological changes which threaten to overwhelm us and certainly make us self-conscious about sex. At this point the challenge to incorporate sex becomes a significant part in total self-development.

"Incorporating sex" does not signify two people trying in parallel play to satisfy each other's instinctual requirements. That is mutual masturbation, not sex. Sex incorporates two people into a mutual life that supersedes their individual concerns and reservations. Incorporating sex does not mean doing something *to* sex but allowing it to be what it is, the absorption of two people in common discovery of the meaning of life.

"... sex has become an extremely familiar public characteristic ... We encounter sexual references all around us in such profusion that we hardly recognize any more how an all-permeating sexual flavor dominates our sense of life. ... Sex has come to be accepted and exploited in a variety of ways which, on the surface, seem to have little in common. Not only is sex an activity; it is also a commodity, a symbol of emancipation, a key ingredient in advertising ... But we are still far from being able to understand all the nuances of sex as the relationship of two persons, and of sexuality as an awareness that we are sexual creatures, able to express ourselves through our bodies ... the message has already gotten across that life is sexual ... The proper question is ... how to respond."

. . . sexuality urges us to seek what will make us complete.

... human sexuality has often been described as an eruptive and disruptive force ...

*The elegance and sexiness of the models . . .*

These media of communication merely point out that sex is everywhere around us.

# Globe
# SPORTS

**TUESDAY, JANUARY 10, 1967**  Forty-Nine

## BUD COLLINS

# Cupid to Make
# Hornung Loser

It is sad to see a great athlete slow down, lose his touch, become a loser. The ravages of age are cruelest to those whose performances have made them gods, to such as Paul Hornung—the All-American bird fancier from Green Bay. His admirers believed that Hornung was one man who could go all the way undefeated, but this is not to be: Paul Hornung is getting married.

The announcement of Hornung's engagement to dark haired Patricia Roeder left his fans in shock. Could their man lose his ability to scramble at 31? Where had the Golden Boy's breakaway moves gone? Was such a player to be brought down at mid-career,

PAT ROEDER

in the bloom of bachelorhood?

For several years Hornung has led the National Football League in scores, some of them on the football field. An extraordinary halfback for the Packers, he made his name as a bird-hunter, an activity he described in his memoirs, "Football and the Single Man." He wrote that though he may be handsome, "what I think the girls really like about me is my charm." This sounds like an excerpt from the "Memoirs" of Giovanni Jacopo Casanova, the 18th century Paul Hornung.

N.F.L. historians point to the time that Hornung nearly—and unwittingly—caused a revolt on another team, the Giants. In 1963 there were rumors of a trade between the Packers and Giants—Hornung for Del Shofner. Coach Allie Sherman stood before his Giants and told them, "I wouldn't trade Shofner for Hornung—and all his girl friends."

An antagonistic rumble of voices shook the room. "Wait a minute, coach," screamed Mo Modzelewski, a tackle. "Let's take a vote on that." Now Miss Roeder has made a Hornung package deal impossible.

For years, bookmakers have set the price at 10 to 1 that nobody would ever run Hornung straight ahead, down an aisle. There's no daylight at the end of an aisle, and Coach Vince Lombardi always instructed Hornung to run for daylight. Miss Roeder has registered the biggest upset since Lilly Damita became Mrs. Errol Flynn in 1940. Flynn also was 31, which may be the age when these players begin to fall apart.

These are hard days for American sporting heroes and their young followers. To kids who want to grow up to be swingers, the prospect of monogamy for Hornung is as painful as the threat of jail for Bobby Baker and Adam Clayton Powell.

Still, everybody wishes Paul and Patricia much happiness. Perhaps it was in bad taste for her to make public the Super Marriage now, stealing a play from the sacred Super Bowl. But when a girl wins over such odds, she deserves notice.

Coach Lombardi did not use Hornung in the Packers' championship victory over Dallas, and he probably won't put him into the Super Bowl. Lombardi is both perceptive and sentimental. He realizes Hornung must be washed up as a get-away runner, and he wants to save him for the honeymoon.

The mass media and their sponsors are far too sensitive to commercial success . . .

Parade, Art Director—Tony Larotunda; Photographer—Ray Solowinski

# Parade

### The Boutsbrar Times

**AN AMERICAN CHILD IN WAR-TORN SAIGON**

An Unusual Prison Experiment:
**FREE MEN BY DAY, CONVICTS BY NIGHT**

AT THE RESORTS:
NECK-HIGH IN
AFRICAN PRINTS

November 6, 1966

Sexuality forces each person to assess his personal identity by appraising how able he is to share himself with others without losing his sense of independence.

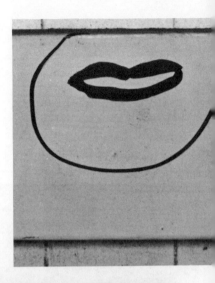

*Little is said about the technical qualities of the car.*

. . . we may ask why we cannot afford to live like this.

The unconscious mind generates vivid and specific fantasies of how sexual urges could be satisfied. . . . The irony . . . is explicitly clear in the Playboy Clubs.

In our time we sense more and more the profound importance of intimate living together . . .

# CHAPTER II

# AUTHORITY OVER SEX

WHO TODAY knows what *authority* really is? What kind of authority could clear up confusion about sex and effectively regulate sexual behavior? In our day there is much heated discussion of the nature and function of authority. We fear that traditional authorities—Gods and parents, for example—have lost influence while formerly unknown authorities such as public opinion polls have come to wield immense power. We are inclined to give backing to the established and necessary authority of teachers and policemen yet hesitate to be authoritarian and rigid in bringing up our own children. We clamor for stronger law enforcement, for clearer guidelines for behavior, but would not want to accept dictatorial power in government, industry, or unions. In short, we sense with some apprehension a subtle shift away from clearly established and unquestionably respected traditional authority to a vast complex of merely relative and openly contested authorities.

For present purposes authority may be defined as that person, circumstance, or philosophy powerful enough to initiate and enforce outlooks or action. Once a broad and general definition of the nature of authority has been accepted and applied to the specific area of sexuality and sex, a further distinction is needed. There is a vast difference between external and internal authority. The former exists in the guise of a divine decree or society's law regardless of how one happens to feel about its worth or logic. Internal authority, however, arises from a person's or group's reasoning or conscience. Nowhere is the difference between external and internal authority more apparent than in the area of sexuality and sex; nowhere are the limitations of both kinds of authority more obvious.

In the face of recent increases in "sex crimes," the well-meaning citizen asks for more stringent laws and more effective police protection. But no sooner has he made his request than he finds himself contradicted by sophisticated experts who indicate that sexual misbehavior is a disease which should be treated through rehabilitation of the sex offender rather than aggravated by imprisonment or dismissed by execution. Disturbed by the lax attitude of young people toward sexual propriety, by suburban lust for promiscuity and spouse exchange, or by the skyrocketing divorce rate, many of us yearn for a clear word of authority. We look wistfully to religion, the sciences, or professional experts— physicians and lawyers. But the very same authorities from whom we expect definitive guidance assure us that the complexity of living among contradictory evidences and symptoms makes it virtually impossible to establish or enforce any simple guidelines for sexual behavior.

It seems self-evident that society has the right and the need to defend itself against the destructive actions of social undesirables. But this brings up the interesting question whether the function of authority over sex should be only restrictive and negative. It could well be that in trying to protect society from those who do not live in accordance with its norms and customs we are suppressing freedom of sexual expression and the creativity of discovering new sexual norms and attitudes. Later on, therefore, we shall have to ask ourselves whether there is not a positive function of authority in matters of sexuality and sex which could provide an orderly and constructive environment for the achievement and protection of sexual maturity.

It is rather intriguing that most of us, when we reflect on sex and authority, immediately envision a restrictive authority which is against—not for—sex. Although not wanting to be labeled prudish or "Victorian," we still suspect sex as an animalistic affair, a brush fire which needs to be quickly contained and then extinguished. Nature, concerned with the survival of its species, including mankind, has in fact linked procreation to perhaps the most demanding instinct, the sexual. Other instinctual needs such as sleeping and eating can be satisfied in individual privacy. But sexuality drives man out of himself and in search of a partner with whom he interacts most intimately and, often, least rationally.

If authorities succeed in regulating public sexual behavior through norms, customs, even laws, it still remains almost impossible by external authority to dictate private sexual attitudes and behavior within the boundaries of matrimony and the home. Yet it is precisely in the family that sexual maladjustment and consequent misbehavior originate. The disturbing truth that one out of four marriages ends in divorce is attributed by marriage counselors primarily to an inability to come to terms with sexuality and the demands of marital sex. Too many children grow up in homes where sex is treated as a chaotic outburst indulged by one parent and tolerated by the other. These children mature physically with a deep suspicion of sex; they may well wish that it could be avoided altogether.

Many enlightened leaders of society have insisted on expanded and intensified sex education as a substitute for reliance solely on restrictive laws and taboos. Consequently we have access, depending on our tastes and inclinations, to every imaginable kind of book on and about sex. Sex education manuals range from cute stories about the birds and the bees, through anatomical descriptions of the procreative organs and descriptions of sexual customs of other cultures, to suggestions of specific techniques and tricks to enhance sexual pleasure. All of these writings are, we are told dedicated to the glory and sanctity of a healthy, clean, and sober marriage.

But it is one thing to know practically everything about how sex functions ideally and naturally and quite another to incorporate such views and insights into one's self-understanding and behavior. Adolescents, for instance, have learned a great deal about sexual techniques and satisfaction. They seem, nevertheless, quite bored with the information, and they persist in demanding that they be allowed to find out for themselves what sex can mean to them personally and how they can arrive at a sexual style and behavior all their own.

Obviously we live in a time of rapid transition from clear-cut, established, and accepted external authority to the relativity of personalized sexual behavior. The weakening of external authority goes hand in hand with a widening of sexual stimulation and sophistication. To face this change confidently and creatively we will have to strengthen our personal ability to come to terms with our sexuality and our sexual behavior. In other words, we will have to learn to incorporate sexuality into our total self-awareness and to incorporate sexual behavior into the whole orbit of our social interactions. In order to appreciate the task, let us investigate how the traditional external authorities have approached sex and how effective they are today in controlling sexual behavior. Consider the present state of seven authoritative forces which, at least in the past, have made deep impressions on society.

## THE AUTHORITY OF RELIGION

No student of religion can fail to recognize that all religions in all cultures, from the primitive to the civilized, have drawn definite connections between man's religious self-evaluation—religious understanding of his world—and his sexuality and sexual expression. The human experience of sex pinpoints the intersection of two insights. One is that he has to leave behind the home of his birth and childhood to find a new identity in married life, symbolized and effected by sexual union. The other is that potency and creativity can either unleash chaos or bring about constructive order. Sex is located between inherited order threatened by chaos, and new order arising from chaos. Sex without the ability to lose one's self grows stale and monotonous; sex without order runs rampant and ends in destructive futility.

The Judeo-Christian tradition has answered the challenge of chaos represented in sex by rendering all of creation in an analogy to the family. The father God who creates order out of chaos, jealously demanding that His commandments be obeyed, universalizes society's needs and norms, investing them with absolute authority. The father-God undergirds and empowers social mores with the full potency of religious symbols, feelings, and convictions. In his role of provider, the earthly father blends divine authority with the voice of society, thus lending further weight to society's demands.

Through the notion of the motherly, represented by mother-church and the earthly mother, the oppressive harshness of the father is mediated and mitigated. The mother understands, explains, and forgives without undermining the order and purpose established by the father. The role of the child is to accept and participate in the universal order of the religious family. In its teachings and rituals the Judeo-Christian tradition combines the universalization of the family with a familial structuring of the universe. A happy, universal family of God, linking the child's early experiences in a human family with religious understanding of all creation, seems an ingenious and practical solution to the question of order and chaos. No doubt both its concreteness and its universality have contributed to the flourishing of the Judeo-Christian culture for hundreds of years. Yet it also harbors some serious flaws which in contemporary America prompt many serious theologians and sociologists to wonder whether the end of effective religious authority has been reached.

Not that such doubts arise solely because of recent books written about the death of God. Long before Freud, even in the times recorded in the Old Testament, certain rumblings indicated serious tensions among the children of God. Was the tribal God of the nomadic Israelites bound to the patriarchal structure of life in the desert? Was He, as the prophets would have it, opposed to the bourgeois settling of His children in the economic and political independence of Canaan's agricultural way of life? It is more than casually interesting that the religious tension between the two competitive styles of life centered in the question of fertility. Canaan, which the Israelites invaded as the promised land, already knew elaborate fertility cults. Canaanites were dedicated to female deities, rituals acted out in sexual orgies, and temple prostitution. The pages of the Old Testament contain a very slanted and censored rendition of the opportunities and the struggles involved in the clash between the patriarchal faith of Israel and the matriarchal religion of Canaan. A study of the ancient religions of the Near East and India yields a more positive and pleasant appreciation of the alternatives to the Judeo-Christian understanding of fertility.

Beneath the surface of the Israelite religious controversy over beliefs and rituals, however, lay a deeper threat to the mutually supportive religion and family organization of the Israelites. Does the young adult not have to leave his parental family, customs, and faith in order to discover for himself, through his own experience and experimentation, his way of living and becoming productive? Putting the question in this fashion shows us the acutely modern significance of what had been ventilated in the Old Testament through religious imagery. One senses the modern Jewish rebellion against authoritarian religious patriarchy when one considers the number of nonorthodox Jews who helped to usher in the scientific Western temper of the present century. Marx, Freud, and Einstein, among many, were Jews who shared a noted aversion to the orthodox formulations and ritual of their religious background. They insisted that man find out for himself, objectively and empirically, what his potentials and limitations might be. Their scientific mood of critically objective investigation and analysis dominates the education of our children.

The father God and His doctrine of creation lose their authority in an age when neither can live up to the standards of empirical evidence and analytic scrutiny. Least of all are adolescents and young adults willing to accept religious teaching in an area where everyone must find his own way through many sexual alternatives. The new nature of sexuality tends to break, or at least to question, parental authority and filial dependence. Sexuality and sex therefore undermine the authority of the family of God in an age of science.

The scientific attitude alone is not responsible for the leveling of religious authority on the American scene. In this first of the young nations, both religious pluralism and the social subordination of religion have deprived the Judeo-Christian tradition of its power to regulate sexual behavior. The American Colonies were settled by those who in Christianized Europe had lacked the freedom to express and celebrate their faith as they understood it. Neither could they find room at home to expand their human drive for achievement and satisfaction.

The dominant American faith is in a man who can build the Kingdom of God as tangible proof of his being truly loved and blessed by God. Religious liberty and hard work are the basic ingredients for bringing forth the fruits of the spirit. Such a faith stands in marked contrast to the European tendency to unfold huge, speculative systems of theological doctrine; Europeans are inclined to adhere tenaciously to rituals long after they have lost their original symbolic power and immediate significance.

American religious pluralism reflects the deep conviction that every man should be free to worship his God in his own way. It is not so important in this context how one theologically visualizes or ritually expresses faith. What counts most is that he be sincere about personal convictions and live in accordance with them. Needless to say, therefore, American soil was hardly the ground out of which a monolithic religious authority could arise and speak definitively to and for all citizens.

For people who were to turn virgin wilderness into the Kingdom of God and realize the American vision of a "land of plenty" there was little time for play and leisure for self-enjoyment. Sex was the means of populating the country and creating working hands in order to wrest new space and livelihood from the natural wilderness. Undue attention to sex would have disrupted the congenial working relationship of the people of God.

Two hundred years after the founding of the American Republic the vast majority of the American people benefit from an economy of abundance, and a "leisure industry" is booming because many Americans have the time and the means to be preoccupied with pleasure. Man has shown that he can use his resources to build his own earth-paradise. The strict father-God of old, holding His children under His almighty thumb, has been dethroned; man appears to be able to frame his own destiny. The American, without rebelling against religious authority, seems to have emancipated himself from it. Or, as the late German theologian Dietrich Bonhoeffer has put it, man "has come of age."

But has he really? As everybody knows, there is an important difference between an adolescent who feels and thinks himself adult and a mature person who has outgrown his insatiable need to prove himself. If one takes as a yardstick the ability to be mature about sex and sexuality, it is questionable that the American people have reached a genuine adult emancipation from the father-God. What seems to be the case is that the religious community has prematurely turned into a social agency eager to sell its goods and prove its usefulness. Apart from formal worship, the life of the congregation differs little from that in any social club. Through pastoral counseling, discussion groups, and sewing circles the parishioner is made to feel that he is served by God through the church rather than that God is served by him in the church. The fashionable ecumenical movement supports the appearance that all churches are almost the same, so that any Christian can choose his preference according to his taste or the social prestige that he would derive from church membership.

The disappearance of religious authority carries, however, two untoward consequences. One is an unresolved residue of guilt about sexual impulses and aspirations. The other is a missed opportunity for the Judeo-Christian communities to help man mature as a sexual being. As to the first, the strong emphasis on the family in the Judeo-Christian tradition resulted in a glorification of sex for procreation within marital bounds. The churches condemned undue fascination with sex and sexual activity prior to and outside the consecrated marriage. Unfortunately, man's sexual awareness and appetite do not lend themselves neatly to such confinement. The genital sexual urge is strongest soon after its onset at puberty, when most adolescents are not yet either emotionally or financially in a position to get married. The rigidity of the nuptial vows, when one does marry, does not take into account that the hasty promise of holding oneself exclusively to a spouse may cause a feeling of claustrophobia. One may have bound himself prematurely, before he truly knew the self and its potentialities. The religious community, simply upholding taboos against sexual activity before or outside marriage, has no effective means to deal with the inevitable sense of guilt which arises from unrealistic moral restrictions.

The second point is even more important. After repressive Hellenistic influence in its early development, Christianity has continued to rank sexual abstinence and celibacy higher than the holy estate of matrimony. The man or woman who has managed to deny sex and family for the sake of service to God—the priest, monk, or nun—is alleged to demonstrate the highest spiritual achievement. The question here is not whether chastity and celibacy are possible and feasible without imposing unwise hardship on the spiritual aspirant; the vow of absolute chastity is, in that respect, taken freely and voluntarily. The problem is rather an ambiguity, a contradictory appraisal of the worth and significance of sex. One teaching of the churches asserts that, as a part of God's good creation, man's sexual nature is itself good. The other teaching downgrades sexual involvement as mere concupiscence, binding the soul in slavery to the flesh, and overcome only through the spiritual liberation of asceticism.

Ambiguity has fathered a real split. On the one hand, some Christians have ridiculed religious celibacy as an unnatural escape from being fully human. Those who took vows of chastity were usually suspected of being sexually impotent or of being frightened or disdainful of man's full-fledged humanity. Monastics, on the other hand, who abstained from any sexual involvement never had to face the task of refining, rather than denying, the crude instinctual drives of human nature. They could, therefore, be of little help to those who found themselves struggling to arrive at a spiritual understanding of being bound to the flesh.

The influence of religious authority on contemporary American society is noticeable weakened. While the cohesive power of marriage and the family has been subject to stresses, Christianity has only burdened us further with an ambiguous outlook on sex and sexuality. Christian teaching offers little realistic help to the young person who is leaving his parental home in order to find himself and his future as a sexual being but is not yet ready to get married. Nor does the church help married people to incorporate their sexual vitality fully into their total, shared life-awareness. The wish or need for extramarital experience cannot be suppressed by mere moral teaching in place of a complete realization of satisfactory marriage.

If religion has failed us, should we not then treat our sexuality as a natural part of us and let nature regulate sexual behavior? Under naturalism are grouped here, for simplicity's sake, all those people, groups, and philosophies that would answer the question with an emphatic *yes*. They may, as Rousseau and D. H. Lawrence certainly would, have different reasons for being affirmative. They may disagree as to what constitutes being "natural." But all of them would like to remove the unnatural restrictions which, in their understanding, religion and society have imposed, especially concerning sex.

Naturalism, in all its forms and periods from the ancient Greeks to the most recent disciples, has always harbored a distrust of anyone or anything that "interferes." "Nature" ought to be allowed to find its own expression and chart its independent course. That these protests in the name of nature have been voiced repetitively indicates in itself that man is his own gravest threat to the supposedly unalterable progress of natural evolution.

The naturalists, among whom we can count the romantic poets and writers and such scientists as Freud, Darwin, and the Huxleys, saw more clearly than the proponents of religious authority that man must accept his own place in the natural world, play his proper part in the total symphony of all creatures. Freud concentrated on man's facing his own human nature. Darwin attempted to place man in the whole picture of an evolving nature. The romantics lyrically imagined a world in which man and beast would live in harmonious peace and enchantment.

There can be no doubt that the naturalists provided an important correction to the Western world view dominated by the religious notion of the universe as God's fallen creation, or to the idealistic, rational vision of the world as the mirror of a universal mind. A respect for nature and its implicit intention to fulfill itself has inspired the naturalists. They have nevertheless to address the question: How can man be truly natural so as to play his appropriate role in the total interaction of nature? The crucial stumbling block arises in man's self-awareness, which allows him to decide for himself rather than to follow only the instinctual prodding nature has installed in him. The contribution of the naturalists cannot come to fruition until man knows how to fit himself into the evolutionary process of nature.

The shortcomings of the naturalists lie, therefore, not in their misunderstanding or overestimation of nature, but in their misunderstanding or overestimation of man. They have overlooked man's relative independence and potential distance from the rest of nature and its workings. The difference between being instinctual and being self-conscious is apparent even in man's sexuality and, consequently, in his sexual behavior. Animals obediently follow the cycle of mating, caring for their offspring, and discharging them into independence. Man is able to interfere with this cycle. He does not depend on a season for mating, nor must his mating necessarily lead to conception and childrearing. Human animals engage in sexual activities and even conception while previous children are still very young and dependent on parental care. In a human family, the severance of the children's ties to the parents does not take place with as little and short-lived friction as is observed among other animals.

As Teilhard de Chardin, René Dubos, and Julian Huxley have suggested, man has to enlarge and perfect his conscious awareness in order to fulfill his natural function in the total evolutionary process. Naturalism has an important point to make in this respect. Its special emphasis on sex turns out to be more meaningful than we have been willing to admit. In view of the breathtaking breakthroughs which the human mind has accomplished in one generation, we have been overawed by what we can do but have forgotten what we are. There seemed to be no limit to what man could do when he put his mind to it. No problem or obstacle ap-

peared to be insurmountable if only scientific and technical inge-
nuity were given a chance to work on it.

But we have overlooked the cost; a technical advance has been
gained at the expense of emotional development. While overheat-
ing his brains, Western man in general, and the American in particular, has remained emotionally underdeveloped. More often
than we would wish, we meet highly trained, skilled specialists
who, as human beings, are neurotic and primitive. Since their
total personality has not been integrated, their abilities represent
a dangerous tool in their hands; they neither know themselves nor
sense how to control their destructive tendencies.

To Freud's great credit, he recognized how closely sex and
human self-awareness are interrelated. He also saw that neither
sex nor self can mature in a person who is not willing or able to
face his own past. Although one cannot escape into the past, an
undigested past forever throws shadows and roadblocks into the
path of the future.

Both sex and self are not specific organs but arise at the point
of interaction between the several aspects of personality. Neither
sex nor self is a thing that can be scientifically isolated, measured,
or reproduced in the test tube. Rather, sex and self are momentary flashes in which man recognizes himself for what he is when
confronted and involved with another. What he is in this moment
of self-awareness depends on what he has become during his past.
We do not want to suggest an airtight determinism. Humans experience themselves as free in their choice and decision making,
although a clever analyst may be able to pinpoint contributory
factors due to heredity and acquired tendencies. Man feels relatively free while he is relatively determined.

Self-awareness can be accepted and deepened, or suppressed
and rejected, by man. He is, to a degree, master over how much
he cares to know and acknowledge about himself. The suppressed
or repressed aspects of personality do not go away. They fester in

the unconscious and interfere with attitudes and actions when such interference can least be afforded. Sex is the most significant of all human engagements, bringing into play the darker aspects of our personality when we are most nakedly and defenselessly involved with another human being.

Naturalism is correct in stressing the importance of feelings. Either we are at ease with our bodily existence or we fear, if not hate, our constitution and characteristics. Then we flee from intimate contact and suspect anyone who would like to come close to us.

The naturalism of a D. H. Lawrence is less than adequate at the point at which it assumes sexual union to be so powerful that the experience of it can overcome self-consciousness in an orgiastic whirl of losing oneself. Not that moments of utter self-abandonment in sexual ecstasy cannot happen. But we are foolish to believe that we can build our self-appreciation or a lasting interpersonal relationship on the basis of such momentary ecstasies. Neither does it avail to blame modern living, its gadgets and time schedules, for the inability to be more relaxed than we are. If romantic naturalism pretends that we would inevitably be more happy and peaceful if we could live in a more rural and simple surrounding, it misleads us. The decisive opportunity does not come to us from the outside, but must originate from within, from our attitudes and expectations.

Naturalism tends to forget a peculiarity of the human animal which none of his relations in the animal kingdom shares, at least before it has been domesticated by man. A wild animal is very careful to stay as close to its place of feeding and safety as necessary in order to assure its self-protection. Man, however, is prone to overextend himself. He is tempted to satisfy his hunger for self-aggrandizement by possessing and controlling as much of the world around him as possible. He overrides the physical and emotional warning signals of his system with pep pills and other stimuli. Having overworked his limited resources, he then tries to quiet down by taking sedatives. As his sex life is bound to remind him, he has alienated himself and has become unable to be relaxed with his mate.

Naturalism constitutes an important corrective movement. It tries to remind man that he is a physical creature and thus an integral part of nature. It wants us not only to become more natural through accepting ourselves for what we are but to come to ourselves through becoming one with nature. Therein lies the weakness of naturalism. As with most corrective movements, it overemphasizes its particular concern at the expense of a more comprehensive and realistic assessment of human existence. Naturalism cannot be a dependable external authority if it does not seriously take into account who and where we are in our life situation. It is not easy, if possible at all, for the American people to forsake instantaneously either their overheated rationality or overactivated technology. We must find ourselves through a broadened and heightened self-awareness instead of reducing ourselves to an unnatural kind of animal.

### THE AUTHORITY OF UTILITARIANISM

Why can we not simply use sex as one of the pleasures of life and let our enlightened self-interest regulate our sexual behavior? If we want to discover what sex is, we cannot evade this very reasonable question. Since sex is such a delicate private matter, it would perhaps be best to let each man decide what he wants to make of sex. His enlightened self-interest will guide him. He will find out for himself how he wants to handle his sexual activities and how much liberty he has under the limits society sets for him. Society will not only discourage inappropriate behavior and deviancy but set norms of public behavior. Especially in the light of so much writing and discussion about sex, one might well conclude that the less said about sex the better. Why should we not trust an individual's or a couple's initiative and decency in managing their own sexual affairs?

Such a utilitarian argument could be summarized as: The authority over sex which governs least, governs best. Unfortunately in the present situation this utilitarian approach to sex is utterly inadequate. The plain fact is that people are not reasonable and enlightened enough regarding sex to warrant leaving them to their own devices. The automatically self-regulating society is as much a hazy myth as is the dependable father-God with His enforcement of bourgeois social customs. In the case of religion, the question is whether people can depend on an external, divine authority. In utilitarianism the question is turned the other way. Can the external social authority depend heavily on the people?

The reason people, sex, and society cannot be trusted to take care of themselves lies in traditional misunderstanding of all three. People are not basically and predominantly rational, certainly not when it comes to sex. Sex is not a mechanism prepared or easily induced to take care of itself. Society is not a structured group of well-meaning people but a conglomeration of diverse individuals and groups, governed and tentatively brought together by temporary common interests.

The utilitarians harbor a vision of the development of man individually and corporately, which must be our goal. Utilitarianism is not mistaken in looking toward man's further evolution. Its mistake has been to take for granted that man has already reached a higher level of development than he actually has. Naturalism also has rooted its attitude toward sex in the assumption that the future has been already realized in the present. What would be the characteristics of a society which, at least in its sexual actions, could be self-regulative? Leaving aside all wishful thinking, we must admit that the sexual urge and the attitude toward life which it symbolizes are not altogether constructive or peacefully harmonious. Sexuality keynotes man's general desire to get what he wants, to conquer what he desires. This expansionist drive constantly brings him into competitive struggles with others. Whoever stands in the way of his acquiring the object of his lust assumes the role of an enemy. As long as a person thinks his sexual fulfillment dependent on external opportunities, he will resent and fight anyone or anything that seems to bar him from finding his fulfillment.

Only those people who either have found sexual satisfaction or no longer seek it outside themselves and their home would qualify for the role of balancing their self-interest with the welfare of others. Hence a mature person is required. He (or she) would have accepted his own sexuality, with its potentials toward an enriching experience and its dark tendencies toward competitive destruction of self or the sexual partner. Such a person would have incorporated sex into his self-awareness and his attitude toward others. In short, he would have learned to appreciate sex for what it is and to see beyond his private wishes and desires to the welfare of the corporate social life. A sexually mature person knows that sexual guidelines for ordering sexual behavior crystallize out of personal and interpersonal experience long before they have to be formulated as social norms, taboos, or laws—and hopefully without their having to be so formulated.

As soon as man tries to use sex as a private pleasure, exclusively directed toward his self-centered enjoyment, he learns that sex loses its significance. Even when more and more sophisticated stimuli and exercises of sexual excitement are added, sex, taken as a mere individual delicacy, grows sterile and boring. Any possible number of variations on sex for its own sake in the end amount to a resigned, disappointed recognition that, because of one's stubborn fixation on sex as pleasure, one has missed the meaning of sex as the expression of love. Sex is not a promise of what and how much one can get from one's environment. It is the indicator of how far one has come in making peace with one's personality and expectations.

As for the authority of a self-regulating society in matters of sex, the record speaks for itself. One recalls the president of a girls' college who, when reminded by some apprehensive parents that she was acting *in loco parentis,* retorted—no doubt with her long experience in mind—that before she could attempt to be a mother to over a thousand girls in a large metropolitan area she must first know what their more than two thousand mothers and fathers really wanted. In an age of thorough relativity it is time that we stopped referring to society, the American society, even the middle class or the white Anglo-Saxon Protestants, as if there were any specific, clear-cut identity to such labels. In a time when many boys look like girls and many girls pride themselves on being less feminine than many boys, societal rules can hardly be expected effectively to control their behavior, least of all their sexual behavior. If parental authority has failed before the young leave home, the authority of society stands no chance of doing better afterward.

But we should not blame adolescents for having single-handedly abolished the chaperone-authority of society. Such a view would presuppose that, before youth's victorious onslaught, adult society was made up exclusively of mature people who had nothing more on their minds than the sexual innocence and virginity of youngsters. Whether we like to admit it or not, regardless of the extent to which we may respect society's authority in matters of sex, sex and sexuality have become a commodity which is being marketed successfully by the mass media, publishers, and advertising agencies. The "oldest profession in the world" has never reached the refinement or the financial success that highly respected businessmen enjoy who sell their products by means of sexual innuendo and exhibitionism.

Those who utilize sex for their mercantile interests take great care to project sexual excitement. If the viewer or reader already suspects that his sex life and partner leave much to be desired, he finds full proof of his suspicions in orgiastic fantasy stimulated by what he sees or reads. When he returns to his mundane life, he is all the more starved and frustrated. He cannot wait to go back to the places where his sexual appetite will be driven to even greater heights of vicarious, fantastic pleasure. This, in turn, whips industry into a still more daring exposure of what sex could be. The varieties of sexual stimuli and possibilities inevitably create a stronger sense of frustration in the consumer, who finds himself in the hopeless rut of his everyday life.

A vicious circle of such proportions can be broken only when most of us are able to free ourselves from the hypnotic bind of believing that the grass is greener on the other side. There are unmistakable signs that young people are resolutely turning away from the slick make-believe world of commercialized sexual suggestion. They want to learn to incorporate sex into a living together which makes sense on its own. Perhaps it is mainly the middle-aged who depend on Playboy fireworks and glamorous sex pretense. Their drab and unimaginative sexual routine at home and their fear which never allows them to be sexually challenged are thus covered up.

In the light of such a fundamental re-evaluation of sex and sexuality, it becomes more than clear that our society does not creatively control sexual behavior. Basically it does not want to.

THE AUTHORITY OF THE FAMILY

Utilitarianism, in its genuine vision and in its undisputable failure, points toward that nucleus of human development, the family. There can be no question that the formation of the most decisive characteristics of a personality occurs in the early years of childhood. Child psychology, clinical psychology, and the experience of psychotherapy—especially psychoanalysis—offer ample proof of this conclusion. Authority begins at home. But parents are no longer sure what kind of authority should reign in the home.

Two or three decades ago parents were urged not to be authoritarian. The child, it was argued, should have a chance to develop his own personality. He should be encouraged to come into his own instead of being prematurely cast in the ironclad image of his parents' expectations. Parents who were themselves the children of authoritarian parents were eager to correct the mistakes committed in their childhood when they turned to bringing up their own children. Such parents played child with their children, tried to be "pal" to their youngsters, and permitted them to make their own choices and decisions. Some psychologists now warn parents of the confusions resulting from too much permissiveness at home. The result is that parents who have learned to listen carefully to experts in child guidance do not know which way to turn.

Let us not, however, assume that the writings of psychologists alone have robbed parents of their sense of genuine, natural authority. The vanishing of the old-fashioned father and mother is far more due to the erosion of independent, self-confident parenthood. Can a man who is daily preoccupied with petty intrigues and competition in paper shuffling at the office be expected to return home with a sense of accomplishment and dignity out of which he can exert leadership in the family? How the father in the family is regarded comes to the surface in how he is depicted in cartoons, plays, or movies. He appears as a well-meaning, relatively harmless, likable functionary. He seems to stand more in need of understanding and comfort than to be a person exuding a confident sovereignty and sense of direction. Home and leisure represent for the father a refuge from the demanding complexities of unending work and obligation. If ever it occurs to him to ask what he works for, all he probably can think of is that he has to provide for the ever growing needs of his family so they can maintain and improve their social status in the community. He too is the victim of the mentality that lives in accordance with what "one does" rather than with what one could be and become. He is ill prepared to assume an authoritative role.

The traditional father-role having been abdicated, it falls to the mother to provide whatever sense of cohesion and well-being the family can muster. She serves as the executive officer, working out to the best of her ability the small and large clashes within the family.

In this role, the mother labors under the challenge of the highly romantic notion that the family is the place where every member's happiness blends into a harmonious nest of together-ness. Captivated and enslaved by the amorphous image of the happy family, the contemporary American mother is scarcely aware what genuine happiness is and how it develops. It does not occur to her that happiness is not an end in itself, but the by-product of the ability to grow as a person. Lacking confidence in her capacity to instill in her family a sense of happiness, she is easy prey to suggestions concerning how to make people happy. Since she feels inadequate and guilty as the provider of happiness for her family, she is easily "blackmailed."

Her children, for instance, are only too eager to detail the con-ditions under which, alone, they could be happy. Relatives, neigh-bors, counselors, and magazine articles oblige by making available advice on how parents should solve their problems. But the more the poor mother reads and hears, the less does she know how to fill the gap between what she feels she can actually accomplish and what she is told she should be doing.

At the heart of the problem of the lack of parental authority lies the strange fact that people become parents before they have become persons in their own right. They tend to get married at a certain age regardless of whether they are personally ready to bring up children. The authority of a parent, however, rests in his stability and confidence as a person, which he then is free to express as a parent. Otherwise he habitually looks outside himself for models and suggestions of what it might mean to be a parent.

Some young people escape the boredom of their marriage by having children. But what these young people at times forget is that children only reflect and return what they sense in and receive from their parents. Parenthood is rewarding when parents can afford to give without depending on a return, when they radiate their trust and delight in life. What has this to do with parental authority over children's sexual behavior? The law says that parents are responsible for their children's actions as long as they are minors. But no rule book tells exactly how to exert this responsibility. In truth, parental authority over sexual behavior is best not exercised by words and rules at first. It establishes itself through a father's and mother's attitude toward each other and subsequently toward their children. If the children sense that their parents live in mutual love and respect, if they witness that their parents delight in each other's company, then they, in turn, will want to learn from and be guided by their parents' experience. At home, genuine authority elicits the children's response of honoring their parents' experience and insights in the art of living. Under such conditions, if the children act in a way that evokes parental authority, there is no need to demonstrate authority negatively through restrictive orders. Parents who hold their children's respect can reason with them, even require certain behavior, for the self-evident good of the family's life.

Technological advances give us more and more leisure time, and counselors advise us to do more together as a whole family. A family which, as a compact unit, experiences the fun and work of living together, they argue, stands a better chance of staying together. But shared activities do not necessarily mean shared confidence. In our strong tendency toward activism we have almost forgotten how to be still, to be aware of ourselves. It is in these rare quiet moments that our life experience can offer wisdom. We need to close ourselves off from the noise and tumult in order to let all that we sense, feel, and are dimly aware of begin to influence our way of life.

Sex is always in danger of degenerating into a routine of release, another one of those things to do and get over with. If parents are to have any impact on their children's sexual maturing, they must share with each other their inner awareness and the meaning of their lives. Otherwise, children grow up with the impression that sex is another one of those adult privileges, like smoking and drinking. They cannot help assuming that they, too, as soon as possible, should gain access to that strange pleasure about which parents are so intriguingly secretive. To adolescents, sex is something that one "does"; as we say so significantly, one "makes" love.

The authority of parents grows, therefore, with their having learned to incorporate their own sexuality and sexual life. They are then no longer driven by external expectations or inner compulsions. Their children learn, without being forced merely to obey restraining orders, that to discover the secret meaning of the self is more exciting than to "have" sex.

We need not be too alarmed about the steady weakening of traditional parental authority. We should also not lament the tendency of the young to find their own way and structure of living. The old family order will no longer suffice. If we do not rise to the occasion, our own sense of worth and enjoyment will decrease and our children will have to go their own way, leaving us, dumbfounded and hopeless, behind.

THE AUTHORITY OF THE PEER GROUP

It should not surprise us to learn, after what we have seen of the American family, that the young gang up to figure out how they are to find their way. Recent studies of delinquent gangs in metropolitan areas have shown that young people, if they do not find structure and order at home, rigidly establish them in their own groups. The charming show *West Side Story* illustrates the strict gang authority and also reveals how difficult it is for a boy who has outgrown the need for the gang to graduate from it.

Peer group pressure to conform to a certain way of living is certainly not limited to adolescents. The so-called young adults—couples in their twenties and thirties—establish an equally stringent code of what "one" does. Even older people look both ways before they decide how to dress, where they dare to be seen, and how much they can go their own way. Any insecure person will keep close watch over how he appears to others and how well he is liked by them. He will be most sensitive to the judgment of his peer group. The peer group need not be restricted to the same age level. It can be defined by factors such as wealth, social standing, or educational association.

Since the members of the peer group try hard to act and look alike, the authority of the group cannot force on the individual a different behavior from that which already characterizes him as a part of the group. On the contrary, their stressed likeness makes it difficult for him to differ from them. External authority is not vested in a person, like God or a parent, nor in an institution, like the government or the administration of a school or corporation. The peer group represents the pressure of equals who do not approve if one differs from them.

In popular usage, mention of the peer group in connection with sex usually refers to the adolescent in his middle or later teens. We visualize a relatively small group of boys and girls who together try to figure out what sex is really about. They are not necessarily experimenting on each other; they may just be comparing notes through conversation. The advantage for the individual boy or girl is obvious. Each learns from the insights and experiences of others without having to find out for himself the hard way.

The disadvantage, however, stems from the peer group's lack of clear authority. Since these boys and girls are brought together by their being relatively the same, no one can speak with more authority or expertise than another. None can evaluate anything that is said or suggested with the confidence of one who is familiar with alternatives. The adolescent peer group originates in the fear of being different from, and inferior to, the peers. Assuming that difference inevitably spells nonacceptance by one's peers, a fate imagined by many as worse than death, the young person tries to conform.

The adolescent acts very much like the nice old lady who insists that she cannot possibly know what she is thinking until she hears herself saying it. Weaving between parental expectations and his own feelings, the teenager is not sure he knows who he is until he finds out how he stacks up against his peers. He does not question the wisdom of having his personality become crystallized from the outside in. First he tries to find himself in comparison to others. Then he tries to acquire confidence that he is who he seems to be.

Finding oneself through comparison with peers does entail serious hazards. No person is identical to any other. However hard we try to conform to the last detail, we still cannot be certain that we are actually what we appear and wish to be. How are we to know for sure that the others with whom we compare ourselves are at heart the way they appear in public? We may try to copy them only to find out that they have changed in the meantime. In the area of sex and sexuality, as in the famous fishing tales, wishful thinking and actual facts are so strangely mixed that no one should seriously measure himself by what is presented as the other's prowess. Napoleon's dictum that no one is a hero in the eyes of his valet is closer to the truth than most of our make-believe.

The peer group cannot be an external authority in the sense of effectively controlling and enforcing specific sexual behavior. It has neither the legislative power of the government nor the justified claims of the family. Its authority lies in the peer group's insistence that a young person come to himself as a corporate being through involvement and interaction with others. The benefit of the peer group arises from its open discussion and experimentation in corporate living through which new ways of behaving can evolve. But this beneficial aspect depends on the members' willingness to be more than conformist sheep.

Contemporary adolescents give us reason for optimism. Sensing the relativity of existing structures, painfully aware of an older generation's confusion, they begin more and more to act and interact on their own. The silent and the beat generation have been followed by a sober, critical, curious group of young people. If they were encouraged and challenged by their elders, they would evince an even more decidedly positive outlook and behavior.

Peer groups are actually tentative and informal minority groups. This helps explain why adolescents are eager to identify with and take up the cause of other minority groups. They feel that in a society governed by power and privilege the established majority will always resist the birth pains of change to tomorrow's way of life.

The adolescent peer group has therefore the potential authority to tell its seniors something about the shape and nature of the future, however vaguely conceived it may be. The exchange might actually bring about a refreshing mutuality if both generations discovered that they were confronting the same problem. All of us face the problem of vanishing external authority, and we are hesitant to embark on the unfamiliar venture of evolving our own internal authority.

Where does what we have said thus far leave us in our attempt to incorporate sexuality and sex more meaningfully into our individual and corporate lives?

Real change must come from looking no longer to outward help and guidance but beginning to turn to ourselves. We must take seriously the fact that we have come of age. Some adolescents sense and welcome this challenge.

One could risk a guess that there is good reason to be optimistic but little cause for passive complacency. The American people have reached a level of well-being, wealth, and technical efficiency which frees them from having to concentrate exclusively on earning a daily living. The most urgent need for a breakthrough lies not in the area of organizational skill, or economic and technical improvement, but in the area of developing people who are confident in utilizing what they have. The glorious activism which characterizes Americans and explains their fabulous success appears here more as a handicap than an asset. We often are tempted to do something quickly, to organize an action program before really knowing where to begin and toward what end to labor. When it comes to incorporating sex, the procedure must be reversed. First we must know more about human development as it pertains to sex. Then we must focus sharply and without distraction on our goal. And finally, we must be willing to concentrate on changing ourselves more than our environment or situation.

# CHAPTER III

# SEX FROM BIRTH TO ADOLESCENCE

No DOUBT the present generation knows technically more about sex than any preceding generation. Public and university libraries contain scientific reports on the sexual behavior of practically every culture known to man. Surveys and statistics cover the sexual activities and opinions of the American male and female. Psychoanalytic books and papers probe the sexual origins of neurotic behavior, inhibitions, and fixations; the same sources point out how adolescent and even adult self-understanding and interactions are affected by unresolved infantile problems of a sexual nature. Novels, plays, and movies overflow with sexual connotations, symbols, and endless conversation on sex.

But with all this study material at hand, each individual must still find out for himself what his own sexuality means. No one can figure out for anyone else how to grow so that sex can be a harmonious expression of participation with others in life. Incorporating sex is a personal task, and identity cannot be separated from the incorporation of sex.

Freud persuaded us that human sexuality plays a role not only in man's individual growth but even in his interaction with others from birth on. This is such a momentous recognition that we still have trouble fathoming it. Psychoanalytic jargon—*Oedipal, phallic,* and so on—does get thrown around. But the popular notion is far from dead that sexuality begins to raise its ugly head in puberty and poses a problem essentially only from adolescence until marriage. Childhood and the later years of marriage, it is sometimes assumed, are the phases of human life when sex is either not yet existent or no longer troublesome.

Moreover, and partially because of Freud, sex is still thought of as a drive or habit, if not a compulsion. In any case, it is considered either an intruder in an otherwise stable and serene life or a toy with which to playfully forget the otherwise boring routine of daily duties. It is difficult to accept that we *are* our sexuality and that sex is an integral part of our living with others. Strange as it may sound, we are not ourselves apart from our sexuality. Sexuality dominates interpersonal relations whether or not we are conscious of it. We cannot neatly distinguish between the times when we "have sex" and other times when sex has nothing to do with relating to others, for the latter times never occur.

A critical reader may suspect that this book is preaching pansexualism or that the author is one of those people who seem unable to think or talk about anything but sex. The actual aim is quite the contrary. The hope is for an incorporation of sex into life-awareness which will make it unnecessary and obsolete to be either for or against sex. Contemporary preoccupation with sex is mainly a strong reaction to the Victorian effort to silence sex into practical nonexistence.

Knowing something about human development, we cannot assume that sexuality develops as automatically as a liver or kidney grows if there is no interference with physical maturation. Precisely because self-awareness and sexual unfolding are so intimately connected, we need to become aware of being sexual beings as we progress in self-understanding. What should never be forgotten is that man, unlike a plant or a fish, matures only to the extent that he realistically becomes aware of himself. This growth in integrative awareness is not limited to especially sensitive, reflective minds but constitutes a natural and essential aspect of human development.

Since we are so prone to misunderstanding sex as being separate from personal identity, it seems wise, in this and the following chapter, to include a discussion of the impediments that may lie in the way of incorporating sex. Thus perhaps it will be possible to expose the mistaken assumption that sexual deviances and shortcomings are by definition alien to normal development. If we believe that people can be divided sexually into the normal, like ourselves, and those few unfortunate others, we uphold a sexual segregationism. Much like its racial counterpart, sexual segregationism indirectly causes the very problems it wants to prevent.

By discussing the darker aspects of sexuality and sex life we avoid also a possible glorification of the "right" way of achieving sexual pleasure and fulfillment. Whether out of ignorance or from having read too many sex manuals, we are often more enslaved by what "one should do" sexually than we are free to discover the diverse ways of sexual expression appropriate to particular circumstances. Trying to achieve what is supposed to be sexual skill is a poor substitute for conveying ourselves through sexual play and exchange. Sexual insecurities and peculiarities are commonly regarded as evils to be exterminated rather than challenges to grow toward a better sexual self-expression. Men and women who have had to struggle hard in their lives often arrive at a fuller appreciation of what it means to be human. By struggling together, two lovers stand a better chance of finding themselves than do those who quickly grow bored with the routine performance of the perfect sex act.

This chapter deals with sex in the context of the family in which one is born and grows up, and which one gradually leaves behind. The next chapter will discuss sex within the new family created by courtship, marriage, procreation, and sexual partnership after the children have gone their way. The break between the chapters may appear to be arbitrary, if not capricious. It allows, however, for a clearer grouping of both promises and problems of sexual growth on the different age levels. The discussion will begin with a consideration of practices and feelings that indicate the severity of the challenge sexuality presents to each person, then go on to scrutinize typical sexual development.

Not all that will be said about sexual frustration and pains lies on the same level of severity nor is everything that will be mentioned equally problematical. The reader may think he perceives a moral disinterestedness or the absence of a sense of differentiation when it comes to sexual suffering. Conscience is distinguished from amoral indifference, however, not by the quantity of moralism but by the degree to which one is aware of the impact of one's attitude and actions on others. The goal of this discussion is neither to extol nor to explain away any amount of sexual suffering. The reason for mentioning it at all is that some sexual misfortune can be avoided, alleviated, or, best of all, outgrown and overcome by a change of attitude.

## MASTURBATION AS A SEXUAL INDICATOR

The degree to which a person can deal realistically with his sexuality manifests itself in his attitude toward masturbation. Although medical and psychological authorities have exploded many of the old wives' tales concerning the alleged consequences of "playing with oneself," social disapproval of masturbation as a sexual outlet remains strong. One need only recall that a standard dictionary definition of masturbation is "self-abuse." It is intriguing to speculate why what, from a medical viewpoint, represents merely the release of glandular pressure should be regarded as abusing oneself.

The concept of abuse probably stems from our religious-moral tradition which insists that all sexual activity receives its justification exclusively within the confines of marriage and procreation. In this view, anything that is not directed toward and consistent with family life constitutes an abuse, or perversion, of the God-given means of insuring the survival of the human family. Man, on this basis, is expected to prove himself as the fruitful link between the generations. If he uses his sexual mechanism in any other way, he abuses himself.

The one who masturbates is simply relieving the tension between his potent instinctual drive and his lack of a sexual partner. All too often, this tension becomes intolerable because of the sexual suggestions which continually bombard him, making it nearly impossible for him to gain any perspective on his sexuality. The same sexual stimuli feed his fantasies of what sexual activity could and should be. Since there are taboos against experimenting sexually with another person, a youth's fantasies substitute for the reality of interpersonal experience and he masturbates.

Masturbation is both more exciting and less fulfilling than a sexual encounter with another person—more exciting because one can give free rein to fantasies unhampered by the limitations inevitably imposed when another person is involved; less fulfilling because fantasies can continue to captivate one only so long as the pressure of the physiological drive has not been spent. The secrecy and fear of being found out which shroud this stumbling attempt at sexual expression indicate that one has not yet grown up to either incorporating his sexual drive unashamedly into a total self-awareness or sharing himself freely with another.

It takes a good bit of confidence to acknowledge the need to masturbate and not degrade oneself for practicing masturbation. Standing in the way of becoming relaxed about it are the many traditional prejudices which come out in the folklore: one who masturbates is likely to become blind, have a blemished complexion, or lose his potency. In fact, the most that can be said physiologically against the practice is that one becomes accustomed to his own speed and manner of reaching orgasm and thus may have more of a problem in adjusting to a sexual partner than would otherwise be the case.

The problems created by not allowing oneself to masturbate more than outweigh this minor difficulty. Rigid denial occurs at the price of the constant strain of a vigilance which keeps attention unduly focused on fighting against sexual urges. It is difficult to imagine how someone so trapped in narcissistic self-preoccupation could give loving consideration to another. Only the person who is relatively at ease with himself can be concerned about another's well-being and happiness.

One's view of masturbation is a dependable sexual indicator of how far one has outgrown the need to prove himself through adherence to self-ideals. In reality, masturbation is to be understood not so much as a problem in itself but as symptomatic of an underlying tension within the person. A chief dilemma of the young person centers in the incongruity between his biological readiness for sexual activity and his emotional unreadiness to assume the responsibilities of marriage and childrearing.

Much of what is called "young love" or youthful lovemaking is, in fact, mutual masturbation. Two people engage each other with the excitement of discovering that there is someone who is accepting, not only of the other's physical being, but of his need and desire to come out with himself. That the partner is similarly gratified forges a bond which may lead both to feel that they were intended for each other.

Older people who have long since married and had families still fondly remember the one with whom they were first sexually involved. The whole mystique surrounding the first love affair, meaning by that any variation in sexual activity from petting to intercourse, is based on the notion that the person who allows one to experience intensively an emotional, instinctual upsurge and release not known before or thought possible is unique. The irony in mutual masturbation resides in the distinct feeling that it is exclusively with this partner that one's fulfillment lies forever, whereas one shortly finds himself eagerly lusting after someone else with whom he imagines that sex could be even more enjoyable.

Mutual masturbation is not without its constructive function. It reveals the possibilities for sexual involvement. By nature, though, it is always tentative and limited. In fulfilling its positive role it cannot avoid pointing beyond itself. It represents a moving beyond the solitariness of self-centeredness in which fantasies substitute for actual exchange. Nevertheless, its focus is still on the self.

The very nature of sex as a corporate experience, based on unself-conscious giving and receiving, urges the partners to outgrow mutual masturbation. This growth process takes many different forms, which can be understood as two variations on the theme. One can overcome the juvenile excesses of self-centeredness through learning to live and develop with another person. Or one can graduate from partner to partner as one comes to terms with his own youthful narcissism. Perhaps a combination of these variations is most common.

Psychologically, the most significant thing about masturbation is its tendency to produce guilt feelings. This activity is an inappropriate use of the sexual organs. It certainly requires little imagination to conclude that the male and female sexual organs complement each other and are intended for each other. Hence, any use of one's sexual organs outside the context that offers them their natural fulfillment, heterosexual intercourse, constitutes their misuse and invites a sense of guilt.

The one who remains fixated on masturbation senses that he must come to terms with what his sexual fantasies suggest before he can give himself unself-consciously to another. But instead of facing up to his self-centered hesitancy to become involved with someone else, he channels all of his desire into a lonely make-believe. His unwillingness to step out of his world of fantasy gives him a sense of inadequacy and guilt.

It is noteworthy that all cultures, like all children, move from an unself-conscious nakedness to a gradually intensified hiding of sexuality. (In popular parlance, the genital organs are often called the "privates.") That this process is gradual indicates that shame connotes a sense of distance and difference. The small child at first does not imagine himself in any other way than as an integral part of his family. But with his growing awareness that there can be distance between him and the other members of the family he begins to notice his independence. He learns to be concerned with himself in comparison with others.

With privacy, however, the child need no longer share everything fully with his family. He starts to censor what he tells and reveals at home. This move away from total integration in the parental family produces both the shame of being different and the guilt of being no longer absolutely honest. Shame is a more primitive emotional reaction than guilt. While guilt stems from the inescapable recognition that one is who one is and has done what one has done, shame signifies merely the uneasy and dim feeling that one is different from others but that this difference could be overcome.

Shame represents, therefore, an unwillingness to be different and to stand up for one's particularity. Out of shame one disowns who he is by trying to identify with an ideal person. Characteristic of such shame is the insecure way a boy secretly compares how his penis measures up to those of the penises of the other boys, or a girl secretly envies the seemingly more attractive shape of another girl's breast.

Obviously it is decisive for a young person's self-confidence and spontaneity how the beginning sense of shame is handled at home. If personal differences and the desire for some privacy are treated as natural and not allowed to disrupt the basic feeling of the family's belonging together, the child will be less tempted to feel ashamed of himself. If he is given the assurance that it is all right to be different without having to feel alienated or rejected, he will be more able to accept himself for who he is.

It is important that the growing child learn the distinction between being ashamed of who he is and being ashamed of what he tried to be and could not quite become. Although the two are related, they are not the same. The second actually arises out of the first. If a growing person is given the impression that who and what he is does not suffice, he cannot help trying to make up for the deficiency. He becomes dependent on external approval, which he tries to gain at all costs. If he fails to do so, he develops the second kind of shame.

In our society, accurately characterized as other-directed, it is doubly essential that a young person receive strong support in his attempt to accept himself. Improvement of character and habit should not be depicted as a substitute for what one is. There is great danger in our eagerness to prove ourselves. Sexually this danger is quite self-evident. A young person who rejects himself, who feels ashamed of himself, will use any proper or inappropriate means to establish his prowess. For his own good, it may be much better that he try to prove himself and learn from his experience. If he does not dare to act out his deep-seated shame, he may turn deviant in his sexual activity.

A person with a strong sense of shame has difficulty in relating intimately to someone he thinks is normal for he feels that he would be rejected should he reveal himself. He fails to recognize that only as he dares to come out of himself will he discover that shame is either the sign of unreadiness or the shield of unwillingness to face human existence as inevitably interpersonal.

Shame is not without its positive function. It acts to restrain a person from being more intimately involved with others than he can afford. We call someone "shameless" who either exposes more of himself than he can do with confidence and ease or intrudes insensitively upon the privacy of another. Put another way, shame-lessness expresses itself in the attitude: "This is how I behave—like it or not!" Basically insecure and rebellious, the one who talks thus cannot afford to be sensitive to others or aware of the impact which his steamrolling behavior has. By contrast, the un-ashamed is very much aware of the effect his self-revelations have on others, but he has learned that without such effect he does not elicit any genuine response from them. This shedding of an undue sense of shame is accomplished only where one risks skipping out of hiding. Confidence in himself and sensitivity toward others mark the person who dares to be unashamedly human.

Whereas shame is associated with feelings of inferiority, guilt refers to a sense of brokenness and separation. As with all ani-mals, the human resists willful breaking away from the family. In distinction from the other animals, the human is aware of this resistance and therefore can feel guilty if his actions lead to sepa-rations.

The question of the appropriateness of guilt feelings centers around the extent to which the feelings are directly related and proportional to the actual deed of guilt. Often the guilty feelings experienced when damaging or shattering a relationship with an-other are perfectly appropriate. At the same time, such breaks may act like a sponge, attracting a host of free-floating, unconscious sensations of inadequacy and uneasiness. Guilt feelings may then be all out of proportion to the objective reality of guilt.

Masturbation is a good instance of how free-floating feelings of inadequacy and uneasiness attach themselves to an act which, in itself, is rather harmless and insignificant. A young person already feeling ambiguous about his relationship to his environment, espe-cially to his parents, can unload his uneasiness and sense of inade-quacy by focusing on his secretive masturbating as the cause of all his problems. Erroneously he tells himself that if that need were under control he would not feel guilty. The full emotional com-plexity of the simple act of masturbation becomes evident when one considers that it provides a welcome, temporary focus for the release of unidentified anxieties and frustrations while simultaneously looming as the single wrongdoing which prevents him from regarding himself as pure.

Sex is the indicator of how well we have learned to live with a realistic awareness of our guilt as the challenge to grow beyond an inadequate self-image. It is really not the awareness of what we are that inhibits our freedom to share ourselves honestly with others, but rather what we think we should be and are not. Usually, we imagine that we would come out with ourselves confidently if we could live up to our highly inflated self-expectations. Since we always fail to live up to our ideal self-image, this failure acts to deflate any confidence we might possess to allow the real self to speak. Hence we become our own worst enemies, crippling our possibilities for growth and maturity.

Guilt is the inevitable by-product of growing up. If one is to become an independent, maturing person, there is no escape from guilt. To grow up is to sever bonds with the family. Guilt is no more and no less than the actual manifestation of this separation.

That honest human existence inevitably becomes guilt laden is no new discovery. Classical Greek tragedy revolves about this theme, expressing it as the human dilemma of having to choose between being only a full-fledged but anonymous and dependent member of the status quo and stepping out of the chorus into the lonely and threatening existence of the one who dares to be himself. Such stepping out is risking all, as the status quo is only too eager to point out. One may try to stand on his own and fall, missing the mark of being able to incorporate guilt into life-awareness.

Undoubtedly, the problem of how to incorporate guilt in a constructive self-awareness has to be faced by each generation, for guilt represents the recognition—however dim—that one has been unable to deal with something as well as either the circumstances or self-expectations would seem to require. In this connection,

Freud introduced the significant distinction between conscious and unconscious awareness of guilt, i.e., the difference between rational comprehension of what is entailed in a failure and irrational unease about inadequate involvement in a situation which we dare not undertake to appraise. The boy who has been told not to steal from the cookie jar, agrees, but goes ahead and steals is consciously aware of guilt.

Freud's notion of the Oedipus complex pinpoints a classic incident involving unconscious awareness of guilt. The boy with incestuous desires for his mother either represses them altogether or quickly suppresses his awareness, because he cannot tolerate even harboring such unacceptable feelings. Although he has no clear awareness of his guilt, he is bound to manifest marked uneasiness in his relations with his mother. The significance of Freud's distinction is that as growing persons we need to come to terms with all facets of our personalities, whether they are pleasant or not. It plainly does not suffice to establish a moral or religious list of sins, encourage people to confess and repent, and then assume that they feel freed from their guilt. Much more important than trying to do away with guilt is learning to live with it as a constructive ingredient of life-awareness.

SEX VERSUS MARRIAGE; HOMOSEXUALITY

Is our usual linking of sex and marriage as rigid as some people's insistence that sex-without-marriage is superior? It is misleading even to compare the two. Homosexuality has become a label for many different but equally confusing sexual phenomena. Literally, the word means sexual attraction to one's own sex, men to men and women to women. But only militant homosexuals battling for social acceptance of their way of life still adhere to this narrow definition. The label of homosexuality is widely attached to all forms of behavior, dressing, and inclinations which do not conform to the images of the "he-man" and the feminine girl. Confusion prevails about what should be called normal, proper, or acceptable and what identified as homosexual.

The confusion stems from a Victorian notion of male and female and from the present-day revolt of young people against such a black-and-white classification. The older generation realizes that its norms are based on oversimplifications but does not know how safely to enlarge and diversify its categories without losing all sense of direction. The younger generation feels that it can no longer adhere to outdated sexual guidelines but lacks the confidence to devise new and more viable ones.

A better understanding of homosexuality could actually help all, young and old, in getting over a deadlock between defense and protest. Once we appreciate what causes homosexual tendencies, we shall be in a better position to envision more promising attitudes toward sex than our present ones. Masturbation offered a good example of sexual shame, the inability to step out of oneself and become involved with another. Homosexuality illustrates sexual guilt, the inability to break away from the parental home and share oneself fully with another person. In a few cases homosexuality is traceable to organic or constitutional factors, but our concern here is with the overwhelming majority of instances in which the ties between parents and children do not allow the latter to grow into independence.

Young people face a disconcerting ambiguity between public estimation of the family and actual family life. On the one hand, church, school, and society praise and emphasize family life as the highest good to which man can aspire. On the other hand, divorce, adultery, and continuous tensions at home speak more loudly than words of praise our actual disregard for the family. A youth coming from a broken or battered home will be more than hesitant to start a family of his own.

Circumstantial homosexuality threatens the youngster who feels that he cannot leave home before he is emotionally released from attachment to a deeply disturbing parental family. Irrational as it may sound, he feels guilty for and implicated in his parents' failure to create a peaceful, constructive home atmosphere. Even if neither father nor mother elects the child as a premature confidant or substitute, he senses that he should help them, though he knows himself incapable of succeeding. This truly tragic guilt breaks the child's confidence about establishing an intimate, heterosexual relationship, lest it lead to marriage and thus to a repeat performance of what he knows and fears from his childhood.

In his attempt to evade an inescapable guilt, he seeks substitute parents and fellow sufferers. To those who seem to promise to be better fathers or mothers than his own were, the searching adolescent will try to play a good, affectionate child. Still, he is bound to act out on them his suspicion and hatred of his own parents, thereby often breaking a relationship that he most needs and wants.

Among his peers, the homosexual finds himself confused by the members of his own sex and threatened by the representatives of the other sex. Seeking an intimate fellowship with those who are most like him and hence understand him best, he secretly idolizes those others who do not seem at all to share his secret pains and doubts. His attraction to his own sex is profoundly ambiguous, while the other sex appears to expect him to be someone he is far from ready to be.

It goes without saying that to the homosexual sexuality is as much a problem as sex is a dangerous mystery. Consciously or subconsciously, he relates his parents' troubles to their sexual differences and power struggles. By being male or female, the child has taken a side and become guilty of being inevitably involved in the home tensions. After being himself sexually awakened, what he seeks most of all is a sexual relationship without the problems he remembers from the heterosexual union of his parents. Sexual bliss and harmony without the pitfalls of a heterosexual marriage is the homosexual's most fervent desire.

If we speculatively assume that such a person could easily enjoy as bachelor or spinster all the pleasures of safe sex without the obligations of marriage and family, we overlook the real handicap of the homosexual. Most characteristic is his narcissistic self-concern. He has not come to terms with himself. Rather, he tries to escape from having to face himself by constantly chasing the one who would make him whole and happy. His narcissism comes to light in his immense interest in his clothing and appearance. His self-concern forces him continuously to seek attention without being ostracized, to be the center of attention without being labeled. But most significant is his ambivalence toward a lasting love relation exclusively with one person. The rate of promiscuity among homosexuals is incomparably higher than among heterosexuals. Likewise, the degree of possessiveness and jealousy is far higher. The homosexual reveals his immaturity by insisting stubbornly that the solution to his life problem come to him from the outside. If his present lover does not offer him what he vaguely seeks, maybe another one will. He overlooks the fact that no one can redeem his own past for him. Since the homosexual love relationship is not sanctioned by society or strengthened by mutual concern for children, the homosexual is ever threatened by the loss of his partner. He desperately tries, therefore, to hang on to him and to prevent his partner's lusting after another.

Much sadness and loneliness reign among those who euphemistically call themselves "gay" while others slander them as "queer." They may actually not be as queer as the marriages and families out of which they have come. The steady increase of habitual overt homosexuality should at least alert us to a basic inadequacy in parental living together. Parents would do well to learn that their sins *are* visited upon their offspring. As parents, we owe it to our children to minimize the brunt of our failures and incompatibilities.

Adolescents, on the other hand, can learn that a painful home situation and childhood troubles prove to be less damaging the more one dares to face them in order better to understand parents and self. They should not demandingly look to the environment to provide them with a more congenial, liberating attitude toward sex. As a matter of fact, it is not so much getting pleasure out of sex that counts. Rather, "incorporating sex" suggests that adolescents can learn to live with each other. The art of living, experienced together, will set the context in which their sexuality will prove acceptable and their sex life natural and lasting.

Legal harshness or social ostracism will prove as futile in dealing with the true problem of homosexuality as will the homosexuals' attempt to lift their impediment to the honor of a superior way of life or their creating their own minority subculture. All of us must mature if the evils of ignorance and deviancy in sexual development and interaction are to be overcome.

## ALLERGY TO MARRIAGE

Why should one get married? Could sex not be enjoyed without the burden of the marital yoke? Could unmarried life not prove even more fulfilling and fruitful? These questions must be seriously faced in a time when enormous pressure is brought upon young people by their peers, parents, and even employers to be normal and marry. A young person who does not want to escape the problems of living alone by the expedient of quickly getting married must brave the raised eyebrows of friends and superiors. Voluntary bachelors and spinsters are not taken for full-fledged citizens and are suspected of selfish irresponsibility. At the same time, everybody deplores population explosions and marital failures!

Certainly our basic view of marriage must radically change. We can no longer assume that marriage is a "natural" institution that is bound to work out well if only the spouses and other people do not interfere too much with its automatic functioning. On the contrary, marriage is the most demanding achievement of man, asking nothing short of total, unceasing dedication of two partners. Furthermore, it is no easy escape from having to make decisions; it requires two people who are mature for their age and willing to give all of themselves to the complex decision making of corporate living.

In the light of this background, why should we marry and why should we limit sexual pleasure and fulfillment to the married? The answer must be that we should not. Rather, we ought to be courageous enough to dispel resolutely many of the romantic illusions that lure young people into marriage and cause them to be all the more disappointed by its realities. The traditional view of marriage as the final permit for sexual indulgence must be discarded for the sake of both a fuller appreciation of sex and a lesser burden on marriage.

If, as we have said, the homosexual is unable to break away from home and jump over the shadow of his past, the one who cannot bring himself to marry cannot break away from himself, nor can he sacrifice his fantasies of the future. He is hesitant to let go of his single way of life, his present obligations, involvements, and advantages. As to the future, he can only foresee curtailment of his freedom, slavery to the spouse or a common life, and troubles which come with the rearing of children.

Actually, one who shies away from marriage is often more clearsighted and honest than his friend who rushes blindly and hastily into marriage because he either cannot see ahead of himself or does not want to think ahead. But for both, the basic question is the same: Is he or is he not ready and willing to be entirely transformed? Marriage asks nothing short of transformation. Can and will he let go of himself, his fears, and his expectations? If he marries, he is in for some sobering and challenging experiences. If he is not prepared to accept their lesson, his marriage holds little promise for success and happiness.

The nature of sexual intercourse pinpoints what we have been talking about. Its fulfillment depends on readiness for utter self-abandonment into the hands of the partner. Sex suffers if it is hampered by a self-conscious calculating of how much one should give of oneself in order to get what one wants from the other. Sex and self-seeking bargaining are mutually exclusive. The sexual pleasure hunter deprives himself of the surprising gift of being more rewarded than one could ever expect. If a sexual relationship is entered with the willingness for self-surrender, it claims the whole person and he finds himself profoundly changed. This experience is suggested by such Biblical phrases as losing and finding oneself, death and rebirth. The question is whether one is willing to lose oneself and find that one is no longer one's own. Genesis, in its earth language, speaks of man and woman becoming one flesh; it conveys the sense of indivisible union. This is the mutual experience of being created anew as an integral part of an inseparable union.

He who would like to have sex now and then, according to his extracurricular predilections and without losing himself in a relationship that claims him more and more, deprives himself of the very essence of sex. He who hesitates to live fully with his sexual partner is merely dallying in a fling of mutual masturbation. Sex claims the total personality without reservations and conditions. Otherwise it is nothing but a mutual release.

The person who sublimates his sexual drive and his yearning for marriage and family into his profession, sport, or hobby will certainly accumulate an immense motivational force toward high achievement in his chosen field. Where your treasure is, there is your heart also. By the same token, many a married man and father who puts his business or leisure-time fancy above any consideration for his wife and children would be better off not married. It is not the legal status of being single or married that counts. Allergy to marriage consists of a hesitancy to be tied down or to give up the freedom to choose as one wishes. For this reason, the monk and the nun do not consider themselves as much unmarried as they see themselves bound to a heavenly bride or groom.

In their resistance to taking up the logical consequences of total involvement, the self-willed bachelor and spinster inadvertently reveal the deepest significance of incorporating sex. To integrate sexuality into a whole awareness of personhood and allow the sexual experience to reshape awareness of life goes far beyond any individual manipulation or social custom. Sexuality is so rooted in the freedom of man as to be either an expression and bearer of life or an exploiter and manipulator of vitality. Man either gives himself to life or abuses it for his own purposes.

Consciously or unconsciously, the one who avoids marriage and family may fear that giving himself unconditionally to life could result in a destructive outburst of those traits in his personality that he suspects. He dimly senses that his careful controls and repressions could be broken down or worn out through the intimacy of living closely and nakedly with another. But in his fear he misinterprets the alternatives.

The choice is not between being irrationally flooded by life and walling oneself off from anything that could possibly overthrow one's planning. The choice is not for reason against emotions or for instinctual orgy against rational inhibition. The choice is whether to curtail living because it may otherwise challenge, or to incorporate sex and all that is challenging because of it into a more encompassing and realistic outlook on life.

The intentional bachelor or spinster should not be viewed as categorically inferior to every married person. The one who need not care for a family and consider his spouse's wishes may actually be free to achieve more and serve the community more dedi-catedly than his married counterpart. To remain unmarried, how-ever, raises at least implicitly the question whether there has been excluded from life and experience elements that would render the person more human and better able to integrate self-awareness.

Marriage not only takes two but requires one to ask for the hand of the other. What about those who never are asked or who are turned down? Customarily we think first of women who remain single because nobody has courted them. Men usually find less sympathy since they are supposed to do the asking. But we should not overlook the man who has invited marriage only to be turned down in each instance. Whatever his fault or mistake may have been, he finally gives up and stays single.

Do involuntarily single persons rank second in our view of human development? Not necessarily! It all depends on how the one who is left single deals with the predicament. Of interest here is how such a person incorporates his or her sexuality into a posi-tive outlook on life. Far from being automatic, the overcoming of undesired spinsterhood or bachelorhood requires constructive ef-forts. Otherwise we would not meet so many single persons, re-sentful and bitter, who make anyone they happen to come in con-tact with pay for their unhappiness. A positive approach lies in the single person's seeking a career that substitutes for some of the missed joys and satisfactions of family life. Teaching, child care, nursing, and social work offer important outlets to maternal and paternal instincts. Enough of our young and old desperately need loving attention and understanding so that no one's offer of warmth and helpfulness need go unclaimed. As richly rewarding as these professions may be, however, they do not and should not be expected to afford the intimacy and continuance of the lasting sex relationship of two people who fully live with each other and care for their own offspring. The single person faces, therefore, the demanding task of incorporating his sexuality without sex.

Some may argue that sex is, after all, not everything. Could not a close and honest friendship, lasting over years, provide the same benefits as marriage without some of the obvious drawbacks of being caught up in the routine and worry of family life? Certainly! We need not even be so puritanical as to exclude the occasional adventure, whatever short-lived pleasure or disappointment it may bring.

What is missing is sex as a sustaining and enduring union with another. Friendship and occasional sex cannot supply the unconditioned challenge of being literally "re-created," made over into a person who can no longer conceive of or understand himself apart from the other to whom he is married.

The greatest temptation that the unwillfully unmarried must withstand is the inclination to escape into external activities. Running away from oneself merely distracts from the central issue. At stake is one's growth from being nothing but sexual without sex to being an integrated person without dependence on another. The sexuality of a single person must not be avoided or sublimated by his working so hard that he could not possibly be aware of being alone. On the contrary, the person never to be married needs to break through his loneliness into the ability to be alone. Jean-Paul Sartre, with his usual insight, said once that if we feel lonely when we are alone it is not because we are alone but because we are in bad company. The question is whether we can stand ourselves when there is no possibility to flee from ourselves. Feeling lonely is not caused by having too few or no companions; one feels lonely when the absence of external distraction reveals that he is bad company to himself.

In this sense, the permanently single person is forced to learn to live with himself to a degree which others may avoid by constantly thrusting themselves on someone else. The one who is married can quickly and easily make his partner the scapegoat of, or the savior from, whatever fault he finds with himself. The unmarried has no one but himself to blame for who he is; he cannot expect anyone but himself to provide the needed remedy.

The single person can appraise his success in human development by the degree to which he allows his sexuality to lead him to himself. By facing himself as a sexual being without sex, he can reach a profound understanding of what human sexuality basically signifies. Reaching that understanding obviously presupposes a finer comprehension of sexuality than the common assumption that it is nothing but the means by which one can have sex. Beneath that crude and actually dangerous opinion of sexuality lies its deeper meaning. Sexuality represents a split within oneself which must be overcome and healed. At the very beginning of self-consciousness a child senses, however dimly, that it is torn between reaching out and holding back, between being aggressive and submissive. Jung has identified this inner complexity as the unresolved tension between masculinity and femininity within all of us. Whatever the labels we apply, the basic tension remains the same. Everyone must come to terms with it if he is to mature. The difference between the person with and the person without a permanent sex partner is that the latter must resolve his inner tensions on his own.

There is a fundamental stress in human beings militating against the balance of the diverse and contrary internal forces. It strains between an ideal image comprised of the high expectations with which one seeks to bolster self-respect and the fears and proofs one has of not living up to personal goals. It saps self-confidence; it prevents realistic self-appraisal. The unmarried may have an especially difficult time arriving at objective self-acceptance since he is likely to blame his own deficiencies for his being left single. He lacks also the advantage of the encouragement and the constructive, loving criticism of a spouse.

The unmarried must learn that it is not his peculiar personality that helps or hinders. Incorporating his sexuality means discovering that through whatever he may think of himself, positively or negatively, life desires to express itself. Personal difficulties are not overcome by constantly staring at them, but by realizing that life never ceases to invite us to stop circling around ourselves. No doubt, the one barred from marriage faces the same task of incorporating his sexuality as does anyone else, but it confronts him with more intensity, less relief. Especially with the unintentional bachelor or spinster in mind, we have now to ask how a person can grow up and learn to incorporate his sexuality.

It has been suggested that masturbation indicates a failure to break out of the world of lonely fantasy and that homosexuality signals an inability to leave behind the parental family. Willful shying away from marriage represents a resistance to give oneself up, while remaining unmarried against one's wish poses the challenge of self-acceptance without help from a mate. Shame demonstrates the hope of not having to be who one is. Guilt stands for the blame one puts on himself for being who he is. In the light of all these impediments and difficulties, how does one learn to incorporate sex constructively into a total attitude toward life? Since sexual maturing is neither automatic nor easy, but demands conscious and concerted effort, what are its key issues and dangers?

SEXUAL MATURING: LATENCY

Prompted by Freud's pioneering insights and findings, psychiatrists and clinical psychologists have furnished us with growing amounts of data on the sexual awakening from infancy to age five.

We know today how decisive the influence of parents, siblings, and other environmental forces is on the early formation of character and sexual awareness. No one interested in human development can afford to ignore these observations.

But curiously scarce are studies of the so-called latency period of the five- to twelve-year-old. As the term suggests, latency covers the seemingly uneventful phase of personality growth between previous and following years strongly marked by swift, often dramatic changes. If we want to know how a person becomes aware of and deals with himself, however, studies of the quiet time of latency may be exceedingly important. Although externally less engaged and impressionable, the child during latency may, behind the mask of disinterest, be digesting his previous experiences and preparing for subsequent involvements.

Sexually, the child has learned by now that he is on his own but has not realized what this means. He is no longer merely Mommy's darling or Daddy's likable playmate. He socializes with his peers and compares himself with them. He measures his worth and promise in terms of how well he is liked by his comrades and how successfully he can stand up to, if not boss, them. At school he finds himself weighed in terms of his academic abilities and his physical coordination. This adaptation and socialization in and beyond the parental family shapes what we call the personality of the child. It is not quite evident what he will be later as a person. But his personality—how he expresses himself in public and responds to external stimuli—grows clearer every day. The child's sexuality is neither in his mind nor manifest in his appearance or behavior.

Important, however, in view of his later attitude toward his sexuality is how well he can bring together what he thought himself to be at home and what he finds himself to mean in the free-for-all of his age group. Since his sexuality will later on bridge the gap between what he believes himself to be when alone and what he becomes for and with another, the latency phase is potentially very significant.

The anxieties and projections of parents have a large place in this phase of development. Not knowing for sure who their child is and how he will make out in life, parents are often eager either to force him into excelling among peers or to protect him from the sometimes brutal competition among young children. Since there are no hard-and-fast rules covering all possibilities, parents and child alike find themselves in a sea of relativity at a time when no one is quite sure about the child's emerging sense of personhood. Yet the relation between a youth's sense of personhood and his externalized personality does determine his later ability to cope with his sexuality. His sexuality is the vehicle by which he combines a free and confident giving of his very self with a sensitive awareness of what he can be with another person in intimate exchange. In latency the child experiments with this combination and tries to balance its two sides without yet being under the stress of strong sexual pressure.

During latency the child begins to recognize that values, norms, and orders are relative and depend on the context in which they are established and viable. His world is no longer made up solely of what Daddy says and Mommy allows or encourages. He experiences collisions with contrary values and norms. He finds himself obeying orders which he may inwardly reject but perceives externally as mandatory if he wants to succeed. The black and white of what is commanded at home gives way to the grayish area of what is propitious at other times and places.

Growing up is far more difficult than a child expected when envying the adults around him. If we hope that a youth will be able to incorporate sexuality and sex into his self-awareness, we cannot overlook the great significance latency holds for the formation of the very personal identity into which sexuality is to be incorporated.

Puberty is well known for its eruptive character. Even the skin of the young breaks out. Body chemistry and emotions and behavior witness collectively to the onset of sexuality as a force in itself. The dominant experience of puberty is that sexuality draws attention to itself to the point of seeming to overrun any contrary attitude or consideration. If one ever needs proof that sexuality creates an all-encompassing awareness, he has only to talk with the pubescent. If one ever questions the need for incorporation of sexuality, he is easily persuaded when observing a boy or girl battling the waves of puberty. In our country puberty is difficult to endure for the young and their parents alike because of our heavy emphasis on youth and our insistence that the young behave as if they were already adults.

The intensity with which the glandular onset of sexuality imposes itself on the teenager is all the more concentrated because he faces this overwhelming force on his own. Preoccupied with himself and what he experiences, he cannot maintain balanced interpersonal relations which would alleviate his feeling of being divided within. His external appearances and contacts bespeak his painful attempts to refute that inwardly he is troubled by sexual fantasies and outbursts. He is torn between compulsively giving in to the urge which so authoritatively demands release and attempting desperately to subdue, if not deny, the chaotic rampaging of his sexuality. He feels lonely because he no longer knows who he is, vacillating between believing himself an asexual angel and a beastly ogre; suspecting both. He actually *is* lonely because he cannot help suspecting any outside person who wants to relate to him.

If someone addresses and takes him for the person he wants to be, the pubescent youngster senses keenly that the other does not really recognize him, let alone understand him. If someone tries to be his confidant the pubescent feels discovered and debased. Sexuality, instead of relating him to the world, seems rather to constitute an unbridgeable chasm. To incorporate sexuality into his self-understanding and his approach to his environment appears to be as impossible as undesirable.

During puberty one cannot escape feeling guilty in the classical Greek sense of the tragic. He finds himself guilty of failing his inner self-ideal and the image he wants others to have of him. Like the tragic Greek hero he cannot win true independence, much less reach maturity, if he does not live through the experience of guilt. If he is to come to terms with his sexuality, he must first recognize that awareness of guilt signifies that he still has not outlived his past self-image and his emotional dependence on the conditioned acceptance by others. No one can achieve ease in being a sexual being except by incorporating the guilt of being distant and different.

Going beyond the mere sense of shame, the young person must recognize actual guilt for what it is, namely, a clash of circumstances with ambitions. Incorporating pubescent sexuality requires that he learn to let his guilt lead him to a more realistic self-appraisal. If he no longer expects himself to be a sweet kid whose fingers never get dirty, he finds that the mysterious lure of sexual self-indulgence fades likewise.

Parents and other figures of authority could, of course, help the young in this painful process toward self-acceptance. Neither high moralistic admonition nor downgrading ridicule is helpful. Often exasperated by the volatile and ambivalent behavior of the pubescent, adults are tempted to tax his self-control beyond reasonable success or to taunt him into seeing himself as a laughable creature of undignified weakness and confusion. What the youngster needs more than anything else is that his elders combine confidence in him with the realistic challenge to learn to live and grow; what is difficult for the teenager to appreciate is that the turmoil of the present is a necessary and potentially constructive presupposition to a relaxed, confident self-awareness in the future.

We would go a long way toward better understanding the challenge of early adolescence if we realized that, psychologically speaking, to grow up means to grow through the so-called homosexual phase. "Homosexual phase" refers to the necessity for the young person to achieve some ease in relating to members of his own sex before he can engage in heterosexual relations. More specifically, he must come to terms with his own body, especially as it compares with those of other members of his sex. Involved at this point is more than anatomical comparisons, physical agility, taste in attire, and the ability to interact verbally with the peer group. A crucial ability to confront and be confronted is at stake here. Mutual sex play with others of one's sex is as much a part of self-discovery and testing as is the freedom to indulge in daydreaming with one's friends. Youth is best described as the time of trial and experimentation. The young person primarily wants to find out how he stacks up in comparison with others of his age group and under what conditions it is all right for him to reveal himself.

In contemporary America there is a great hesitancy to acknowledge the existence of and the need for the homosexual phase. Long before this phase parents and teachers emphasize the child's sexual identity in dress and behavior and arrange social activities on that basis, prematurely forcing him to play-act his sexual identity before he is up to the challenge. Ironically, parental fear that without such pushing a child will not turn out to be a "real" boy or girl creates in the child anxiety over whether he or she can ever measure up to the expectations. Any personality feature which does not easily fit into the mold of what is held to be typical of the normal boy or girl is suspected by the growing youth as evidence of his being odd. If one were to set out to frighten a young person into withdrawal and tormented loneliness, there would be no better way to do so than by teaching him to regard an aspect or expression of himself as queer. The by-product of the fear of being different is that the popular prototype of the American is one who is neither sensitive enough to recognize his uniqueness nor confident enough to express himself spontaneously. He who fears he may be different is driven to search for others who also dare to be different and therefore will understand and accept him. Out of irrational fear of homosexuality, we actually contribute to its spread by promoting images of virility and femininity which not only are unrealistic but serve to stunt personality growth, frustrate free emotional expression, and favor stereotypes of "he" and "she" behavior.

Still more somber is the effect of such caricaturing of male and female characteristics upon marriage and family life. How can a young man who has been trained to suspect his emotions, let alone express them, be tender and responsive as a lover, or gentle as a father? How can a young woman who has been inculcated with the feminine ideals of modesty, submission, and sweetness fulfill the taxing demands of parenthood, which she often must do by herself when the father is little more than absentee householder?

What is popularly called "puppy love" initiates the adolescent into the interpersonal. Few of us have not been overwhelmed by the euphoric feeling of being irresistibly drawn to someone who we were sure was the fulfillment of all our dreams. This sudden rapture is, however, as fragile as it is ecstatic. Though the one enveloped by the feeling is sure that this is "it" and will last forever, the very experience of being transported above the trivia of mundane living would warn the sober-minded that what goes up must come down. The person who is in the clouds cannot be reached by such pedestrian reasoning. The best a friendly bystander can do is to be understanding when the inevitable re-entry occurs.

The mood of adolescent attachments is well captured in the phrase "falling in love with love." As the words of the well-known song of that title continue, "Falling in love with love is falling for make-believe." To be caught up in such a state is really to be ensnared in the experience of an experience, and not to be related to another person; attention is focused more on the feeling of being in love than on the qualities and potentials of the other person. The overriding importance of the feeling of being in love shows itself in the ease and rapidity with which one love object can be replaced by another while the intensity of feeling remains constant. That it is possible so quickly to transfer desires from person to person, all the while assuming that the latest is the love that is here to stay, should give us pause when people suggest that the measure of how much they are in love can be used to decide whom they will marry.

A curious shift marks the difference between infancy and adolescence. The infant couples an almost nonexistent self-awareness with a practically uncensored self-expression. It is never self-conscious about crying when hungry or wet. A child gradually learns that environment takes self-expression as a reflection of how good he is. A good boy, he finds out, does not always cry when hurt or disappointed, while a bad boy is one who throws a tantrum whenever he doesn't get his way. Thus the child learns to distinguish between self-awareness and self-expression. He begins to know himself as sometimes good and sometimes bad. He learns to censor his self-expression, i.e., to know when and when not to show how he feels.

In contrast to the infant, who is long on expression and short on awareness, the adolescent is often painfully self-aware but inept at expressing himself. As a result, there is distance between his private self-awareness and how he appears to other people. Without question, this distance is necessary if he is to develop adult independence, for he first must learn to be loyal to himself before he can be dependably involved with others. What creates difficulties in this time of transition is his unavoidable dependence on his environment for guidelines and the measure of his growth. Looking to an environment for clues as to who he is and where he is going is hazardous, though, since it sometimes prematurely suggests to him a self-ideal limited to the terms of the status quo. The environment can never appreciate, let alone suggest, the potential outcome of *independent* resources.

Since being human means being deeply involved with others, young people feel guilty because they are unable to enter or sustain such relationships. Their dim awareness of their guilt of withdrawal comes out in the question: Who am I to involve another person? Sexual intimacy would involve the whole person. But, since they are not ready for it, yet cannot be comfortable without it, they labor under the guilt of not being fully mature. And they express this dilemma by constantly falling in and out of love.

As exasperating as their emotional fluctuations may be for parents and other adults, the fads, crushes, and ecstasies of young people do play a positive role in the process of maturing. Besides providing a needed outlet for their superabundance of physical energy, these experiences allow the young to test their potentials by identifying wholeheartedly with an ideal possibility. They rightly sense that only through complete and passionate involvement in specific avenues which show promise as ways to self-fulfillment can they ever find out where their genuine inclinations and inevitable limitations lie.

## ADOLESCENT DATING

The significance and function of dating comprise today a very confused issue. Occasional dating over against "going steady" evades clear definition and distinction. It is especially difficult to tell how much sexual liberty is taken in either case. This depends entirely on the partners involved and their personal attitudes. Under the label of dating the degree of sexual intimacy can range from sedate formal dancing in public to sexual intercourse in a steamed-up car on a lonely lovers' lane.

Nor is the contemporary uncertainty about labels for young people's activities limited to the custom of dating. All the clearly defined traditional terms have undergone radical changes. In the past dating, courtship, and engagement were commonly understood terms which carried implications as to how much time was spent together, how the parental families were involved, and so on. In our day two developments have entirely changed the picture.

First, the exclusive attachments of two adolescents have moved toward a younger age. Going steady, getting "pinned," and becoming engaged are not unusual even in the early teens. The age of those getting married has also dropped. Second, recent advances in effective birth control and treatment of venereal diseases have removed former fears of unwanted pregnancy or infection. Adolescents obviously will not retain traditional inhibitions and customs based on threats now effectively countered. But in the transition period between the regulations of their parents' time and the norms of the future it is all the more mandatory that adolescents be as clear as possible about what is involved, and incorporate their sexuality into a total outlook on life and their sex life into a responsible human interaction. In previous times the accepted official rule was that there be no premarital intercourse. For the more honest the question of premarital intercourse has arisen and must be faced. Should we stubbornly maintain, even in view of many transgressions, the rule of premarital virginity? Or should we frankly admit that we cannot hold on to such an ideal and hence abandon it? Does the latter possibility not in effect invite even greater sexual libertinism among the unmarried?

St. Augustine counseled: Love, and out of this love do wholeheartedly what you decide. This ancient observer of man knew that one should search his attitude and motivation instead of relying on external rules. Often young people, to the distress of their parents, unknowingly paraphrase St. Augustine in defense of their desire for premarital intercourse. If we love each other, they argue, why should it be wrong to go all the way? They correctly discern that it is the nature and intensity of the relationship which should decide how sex should function as one of its integral parts. The question is, therefore, not whether premarital intercourse is permissible, but whether or not they love each other sufficiently to include sex in their relationship. The high rate of early marriages seems to indicate that many young couples still prefer to link sex and marriage. But the social, legal, and religious sanctions of their relationship do not rest on its interpersonal quality. We must be clear that sex and marriage are not necessarily linked. A legalized marriage may be sexually intolerable and destructive. Likewise, a sexual relationship without marriage can be interpersonally very satisfying and for both partners very constructive.

The real question to be decided is whether a boy and girl maintain a true love relationship which justifies their being sexually involved with each other, and if so, from what point. And this question brings us right back to the issue of the role and significance of dating. What have dating and sex actually to do with each other?

Basically, dating fulfills a function radically opposed to the binding nature of sex. By dating, the young can find out whether they are at all ready to get profoundly involved with the other sex. At the beginning of a dating career this will probably not be the case. At that time the adolescent needs someone who is simply congenial to his point of view. Often prompted by anxious parents who want their children to be popular, children play at dating before they have any even egotistic interest in the dating partner as a person. But if a young person is not unduly narcissistic he will gradually discover that the exchange of thought and feeling creates a common bond. He will find that with one he is more at ease and can reveal more of himself than with another. Hence he will seek out those with whom he can be as true a person as he knows how to be.

Therein lies the functional significance of dating. It permits the discovery of how much and with whom one can be oneself. Dating must, therefore, by definition be promiscuous. Only through comparisons can the dating process of selection grow to be meaningful. The crucial issue should not be to "have" a date, for social or other reasons, but how to be genuine and at ease with one's date. Only a prude would assume that such dating takes place without generating erotic stimulation or thought or fantasy of sex. Early dating precisely helps to show the adolescent that his world of sexual fantasy is one matter and the reality of interpersonal relations another. He learns, thus, that awareness of one's sexuality is not tantamount to living it out in sex. The difference lies in the degree to which the sexuality of the respective partners impinges upon their dating.

As a rule of thumb one could say that as long as "having sex" is foremost in adolescents' minds and overshadows any other considerations, they can be sure they are not ready for sex. As long as "having sex" is the principal reason for two people's dating they prove thereby that they have not come to terms with their respective sexualities and are not mature enough for sex.

The one who truly loves no longer asks how much he can love the other person. He recognizes, with some surprise, that love has claimed him. He finds himself considering the other person more than himself and seeking the other's joy and pleasure more than his own. If there is any genuine meaning left in our almost completely trite expression "falling in love," then it is the experience of falling out of one's self-centeredness into centering in another person. The one who loves must and should force himself to ask whether or not he could live with the one he loves. This consideration distinguishes loving and being emotionally captivated by someone.

In this light, the question of having or not having sex recedes into its proper perspective. Sexual relations should not be entered into with a person with whom one has not lived enough to know that one can be related without all kinds of makeup. Otherwise sex binds together basically incompatible people who have not dared to face up to their incompatibility. Sex should not be used to smear over, however romantically, the fact that neither dating partner has yet revealed himself or considered the other for what he or she is. Dating serves only a preliminary function in preparing a young person for the more exclusive relation of love. It is never an end in itself or an adequate substitute for a more extensive and intensive relationship. Still, there is no substitute for the adolescent's "playing the field." Otherwise a player may never know either the field or his ability to play. To marry quickly and blindly, out of the fear that one never could play the field, leads only to the later nagging suspicion that one might have done better.

Compared with the Victorian segregation of the sexes it is encouraging to witness, today, the growing social ease of young men and women with each other. In this regard, one could make a good case for the view that young people are becoming more interested in learning to live with each other than in using any and all occasions to develop their sexual prowess. It may well be that the older generations, having lived through the Victorian age of inhibition and the counterrevolution of libertinism, project their ambiguous attitudes toward sex on their children. The fact that sex is still a problem for the older generations does not necessarily mean that it is the same problem for the younger.

# CHAPTER IV

# SEX FROM LATE ADOLESCENCE
# TO MARITAL PARTNERSHIP

FROM WHAT HAS BEEN SAID on the preceding pages it is evident
that we face a radical redefinition and re-evaluation of marriage
and the family. There is little in the traditional form and customs
of marriage and the family that does not deserve careful scrutiny
as to its usefulness when we are about to chart our own course or
ask ourselves honestly how well we are doing in our own marital
or family life. Should we unquestioningly believe that our homes,
regardless of their material and cultural circumstances, bring forth
young people who confidently know how to live, alone or together?

## ENGAGEMENT TO MARRY

Engagement offers the opportunity to discern how and with whom
one can accept the past and move on with confidence to face the
future with all its uncertainties. During this time of testing, it is
most important that a couple find out whether they can give each
other room to grow and change, without losing their mutual
respect. Although the testing pertains to all areas of their actual
and future living together, usually they can best judge their potential for constructing a mutually pleasing marriage relationship
from their ability to achieve unison out of their individual attitudes toward sex.

An engaged couple faces, as its first task, the unlearning of unwarranted, though very popular, notions of the sexual idiosyncrasies of the male and female. It is commonly assumed that the male is the aggressive one, eager to get what he wants, self-confident in his virility, and knowledgeable about all the tricks. The female, by contrast, is said to be passive, hesitant to yield, modest in her femininity, and innocent. Certainly today these stereotypes are anything but accurate. We are becoming aware that all of us are a mixture of healthy, not just neurotic, masculinity and femininity. Contemporary adolescents tend to blur the traditional social characteristics of the sexes. It is difficult to assess just who is being masculine and who feminine when one encounters the long-haired boy and his dungaree-clad girl friend. Moreover, it may be the virile-looking young man who harbors feminine emotions, while the attractively girlish young lady may be hiding the shrewd, calculating hardness of one who wants to dominate.

Quite obviously, there are fundamental biological differences between male and female, and these get translated into expectations about social roles. The male is supposed to be the one who is aggressive, who initiates, who provides for and protects his family. His functional role in a family is that of a decision maker upon whom the other members can depend. The female is usually seen as the more passive, receptive personality, who welcomes and encourages her husband while caring for and nurturing their offspring, initially in her body and later in the home.

Were husband and wife pure forms of masculinity and femininity, it might be relatively simple for them to establish a suitable marriage. But since all men and women embody both masculine and feminine features, a functioning marital relationship requires that both partners recognize in themselves and each other the specific weave and the ambiguity of their individual temperaments. Casual remarks that "there is a child in every man" and "she wears the pants in the family" indicate our awareness that the matter is peculiar to the partners.

The contemporary American way of life adds its own complexities to attempts to express masculinity and femininity in marriage. With the disappearance of manual labor, the male loses the opportunity to prove his strength and dexterity and thereby his confidence in his more manly attributes. With brainpower now the most marketable of his abilities, he finds himself exhausted by the type of work which many women could do equally well. Small wonder that he does not exude much authority as a husband and father. At work he is a small cog in a vast, anonymous machine. He senses that his contribution does not add up to much. His wife finds herself in the position of having to play a manly role. Decisions concerning childrearing and family life devolve on her. In the community she must uphold, if not enlarge, the prestige of her family. Constantly bombarded by the values of an achievement-oriented society, she projects her pride and ambition on her husband, pushing him to be ever more aggressive and successful. In the few moments which the crowded professional and family schedules leave to man and wife, it is almost impossible to switch suddenly to the mood of leisure and relaxation necessary for them to delight in each other and further their common life. All the good reasons, such as the work still to be done or the sleep to be caught up on, lend themselves well as escapes from having to take stock of the quality of a marriage.

It is important, then, that engaged young men and women have the fullest opportunity to find out whether their relationship holds sufficient promise to justify its being made permanent. Often the courtship of experimenting and testing is cut short out of the desire either for sexual relations or for permanent defining of the relationship. Emphasis on going steady when emotionally one is barely out of diapers puts a heavy onus of finality on the official engagement so that young people find it difficult to break up an unproductive relationship.

The decision to get married represents taking a considerable risk. We have asserted that an open-minded, flexible attitude of being willing to consider and struggle with any issue is most conducive to the establishment of a workable marriage relationship. This viewpoint, however appealing in theory, may appear to some as idealistic and expecting far too much of anyone, especially young men and women. Others, willing to pass over the question of the realism of the viewpoint, may conclude that we are offering what we regard as a surefire recipe for marital success.

Both those who doubt the workability of our view and those who treat it as a collection of inside tips misinterpret the intention of this book. Our intention is to suggest that people can develop the resources to grow through actually living together, and that sex is an indicator of how far they have matured because of each other.

Far from painting an idealistic picture of what *could* be or offering a road map to a land of sexual bliss (there are already enough books proclaiming to do this), we are challenging people to discover for themselves the art of living. Living together encompasses far more than sexual enjoyment. Not only can sex not carry a marriage; it can never make up for personal incompatibilities. If young couples realized this in courtship, they would perhaps devote themselves to discovering how much of their respective idiosyncrasies they could tolerate.

Sex, being the indicator of how well two people can share each other, is not legitimated by marriage; it needs no such legitimation. On the contrary, the decision to get married may well be bolstered by what this indicator reveals concerning two persons, ability to be free in each other's presence without insensitively taking advantage of each other. Sex *is* legitimated by the quality of regard which two people have for each other in full awareness of their respective differences and weaknesses.

Any couple contemplating marriage must attempt to see through the make-believe of appearance to the person underneath the mask, who would like to be genuine. Similarly, a couple must explore how well their respective traits complement one another.

There is no absolute law concerning what is entailed in being a wife or husband. But it is crucial to discover what capacity they have for forging their abilities with confidence into a unique marital relationship.

The danger involved for two people who are not very aware of themselves but feel they can complement each other is that in the actual marriage relationship their neurotic tendencies to dominate or be dependent will be aggravated. It is exceedingly difficult to imagine how marriage is made in heaven, but easy to fathom how marriage becomes a living hell on earth.

Instead of leaving the learning of how one can be constructively married to the difficult period of the first months of marriage, those seriously contemplating marriage would do well to work together to demolish unrealistic images, hopes, and demands. By sharing with each other any hidden conditions and calculations which they regard as essential to their future happiness, and without trying to reconcile their differences only verbally, an engaged couple can pierce the fantasies of who they thought each other to be and concern themselves with their actual potentials for a new life together.

Such an honest sharing cannot but be liberating to both. Either they discover that insurmountable hurdles stand in the way of their ever being able to be close and unpretentious together and are saved the pain of constant marital tension and discord, or they find out that their struggling together frees them from any assumptions previously held as indispensable prerequisites to being happily married.

## THE COURAGE TO MARRY

In a casually uttered aside, Antoine de Saint-Exupéry said once that to love does not mean so much to look at each other as it implies to look together in the same direction. As counselors have found out, giving premarital and marital advice is very difficult. The engagement period seems to be such a delightful experience that any mention of potential marital difficulties falls mostly on deaf ears. To the two about to be married his Cassandra cries reveal that the counselor either is inept in his own marriage or has known of too many marriages which have failed.

When the married couple comes with its troubles, both spouses appear to have utterly forgotten how much mutual good will and forbearance they showed before the wedding. The marriage counselor can only point out that the concrete difficulties are symptoms of a destructive attitude. Instead of incorporating their lives into an inseparable, indivisible unity, they have pulled apart into the posture of competitive comparisons. Each spouse insists on his list of what he or she has given and what he or she has not received. They both overlook that marriage is a sixty-sixty proposition in which a carefully calculated addition of debits and credits results in nothing but disillusionment.

The very wording in which the church couches its solemnization of matrimony underscores the inevitable risk which is always involved when people marry. However soberly two people have weighed their chances for working out a life together on the basis of what they know about each other, neither can foretell how he or his spouse will respond to the stresses and strains, successes and failures. Realistically, the most they can do is make up their minds that they are able and willing to take the risk of getting married, and to set forth without constantly looking back in regret or sideways in thinking how much better it would have been with someone else. The temptation to look backward and sideways is always present; marriage partners can avoid responding too eagerly to it if they recognize marriage for what it is and can be.

Young men and women are often misled by the traditional tenet that marriage legitimates sex. Put another way, the counterpart to the cult of premarital abstinence is that after the wedding sex is both pleasurable and a God-ordained right. Unfortunately for young people for whom sexual enjoyment is a chief reason for getting married, they cannot escape taking *all* the risks entailed in marriage. They are bound to discover that sexual activities play a less dominant role in married life than they had anticipated. It is, therefore, misleading if one holds up to the uninitiated the questionable ideal that full and satisfying marital sex is suddenly granted through the wedding ceremony. The ability to respond sexually to another is not magically imparted but acquired through a slow, sometimes rocky, learning process. Given the still existing social taboos on sex, young people, before they can begin to be comfortable with other persons sexually, must first learn to be at ease with their own sexuality.

Quite possibly, what most jolts newlyweds shortly after, if not during, the honeymoon is the discovery that their marriage, which had been thought of as almost perfectly arranged in heaven, has turned out to be a rather hellish earthly trial. This jolt indicates that the couple has much more to struggle with than the partners' adjusting to each other through establishing a daily routine. Little things do appear to mean a lot—matters as minute as who squeezes the toothpaste tube from which end and whether or not the bride cooks exactly like the groom's mother; but they are symptomatic of the need for a far more basic adjustment. Each person coming to marriage brings with him a host of expectations and resolutions as to what the marriage will be.

Having keenly observed the married life of other people, including their parents, young couples are determined and confident that theirs will be a relationship in which true love conquers all. Lurking beneath the surface of early married life is the reef of unadmitted calculation. Each partner figures secretly how much he has sacrificed in trying to make the other happy and what he has received in return. In terms of expectation and investment, few there are who do not think themselves very much short changed.

In feeling cheated and even embittered by how his marriage

has let him down, a person fails to recognize that the unresolved tension between high ideals and the inevitable limitations of married life keeps him in a perpetual state of frustration. So long as one is unwilling to let go of grandiose dreams, the realities of married life will always seem disappointing. The potentials for a rewarding marriage lie hidden in the marriage relationship, waiting to be discovered and unfolded. All that preconceptions and expectations do is to blind one to the possibilities at hand.

Underlying the disappointment that marriage has not lived up to expectations is the attitude that marriage is the team effort of two idealists. Such people need to experience the mutual freedom which comes from leaving behind all previous notions of what marriage should be and permitting themselves to find out what a specific marriage relationship can be.

In married life, the rendering of sex into a shared self-expression is an ongoing process having three stages: establishing a home, rearing children, and adjusting to later life. As newlyweds, young people enjoy the privacy of their home as a place apart from the obligations of work and the interference of the parental families. The more they insist on shutting out the world and giving exclusive attention to each other, however, the more quickly they tire of each other and begin to seek independent activities and acquaintances. The home, previously just a love nest, increasingly becomes a way station for entertaining and renewal of energy. Neither the extreme of withdrawal from the world into togetherness nor complete submergence in unrelated activities allows a young couple to establish its own joint way of participating in the life outside.

As the organism is sustained by the rhythm of constant breathing in and out, so with the relationship of marriage. As spouses share together their respective encounters with the world surrounding them, they are enlivened through joint reflection and can return to their given tasks more deeply aware of their role and fulfillment in common life. Marital sex represents the spontaneous, unself-conscious expression of life's unceasing movement. The legal understanding of marriage as a contract should not be mistaken as obligating only so long as it offers tangible benefits for both. Its meaning is, rather, that two people consent to discover together how they move in their self-understanding from self-centered autonomy to mutual give-and-take without calculation.

Far from implying that two people should collaborate on the steady realization of a blueprint for happiness and achievement, marriage signifies the unconditional commitment of two people to the unpredictable venture of what they may become. Children, in turning spouses into parents, symbolize this commitment, since their characteristics cannot be predicted but their existence demands the wholehearted devotion of the parents.

The question concerning marriage, therefore, is not so much deciding with whom one can pursue the most pleasure and happiness as it is discerning who offers to exchange the most flexible possibility of realizing life for and with each other, in spite of each partner's deficiencies. Sex, in this respect, is indicative of the courage and risk which inevitably accompany the step from self-consciousness and self-concern to full-fledged corporateness.

One might wonder at anyone's readiness to engage in such a demanding relationship as marriage. To be sure, the obvious dangers entailed in a common life permanently frighten some away from ever daring to be nakedly human with another. Others manifest their apprehension about getting married by simply taking the leap and willfully blacking out for the moment any consideration of what the future might demand. Those who forever run from or suddenly plunge into marriage may be doing so because they are dimly aware of the risk involved and are trying to escape or avoid it.

Whether or not a couple can consider candidly the possible difficulties that lie ahead and their willingness to struggle with them is itself a good test of how well they could live together as man and wife. We tend to assume that a good marriage choice can be measured by the degree to which the prospective partners share common interests and tastes, similar backgrounds and values, and equivalent social and economic status. While the statistics may confirm that those who enter marriage with many similarities and few tensions have a greater probability of weathering common marital strains, they have no bearing on whether such a congenial couple can either deal with unusual challenges or create a rich life together.

Far more basic to the chances for marital fulfillment than shared characteristics is the personal resourcefulness of the two spouses. People who can work together on a problem, tolerating each other's idiosyncrasies and criticisms without drifting apart, can develop an intimacy and closeness much more encompassing than merely sexual or social compatibility. Without some assurance of their ability to listen to each other, to reason and learn together, the prospective bride and groom gamble. A certain risk is always there. The issue is whether they face it as a challenge by focusing on potentials to grow together or try to circumvent it by suppressing anything that could create tension, hardship, or controversy.

PARENTHOOD

Because of better means to plan and control parenthood, children are no longer an arbitrary gift from heaven. Parents are beginning to ask themselves how they can responsibly meet their new obligations. Considering the number of children they can satisfactorily support, they contemplate also where to bring them up, what kind of education and training to give them. Much anxious wondering goes on as a parent tries to imagine his child's future.

Parents are often tempted to build their children's world, so to speak, from the outside in. They begin with material resources, educational and cultural opportunities, and end usually with trying to fit the young into a blueprint for successful coming out. They forget that, in the meantime, the growing child has carefully looked over how his parents feel about their own circumstances.

Could we perhaps start the other way around? We might prepare our offspring better if we concentrated foremost on their inner awareness of themselves and their environment. A child who is confident about himself, realistic about what he can be and do, is able to use constructively whatever external opportunities we provide for him. All the complexities of married life, of which sex is an indicator, greatly influence the way parents and children interact. Although to state that a direct cause-effect relation exists between marital sex and childrearing would be saying too much, it is difficult to imagine that unhappy spouses could bring up happy children, or that parents who are frustrated and ill at ease in their own sexual life could impart a constructive appreciation of sex to their children. Discussion in the thorny area of sex education would certainly be clarified if it were recognized that *how* parents communicate with their young on this subject is at least as important as *what* they try to convey. Still more important is what they show in their own conduct with each other. Children are very observant of parental interaction and quickly become sensitized to any discrepancy between pronouncements and performance.

If it is true that parents have a basic influence on children's orientation and development, the reverse is just as true. The mere presence and growing up of children not only disrupts the exclusive intimacy of man and wife but brings into being a new context for living together, the family. In addition to having to devote a good deal of time and energy to thoughtful caring for their offspring, husband and wife change in their attitude toward sex.

Just as their conversations and planning more and more center around being parents, so their sexual life mirrors their having ceased being simply lovers. If there is a tension between their being parents and the desire to be simply lovers, or if, at least unconsciously, they resent the obligations of parenthood, they would do well to scrutinize what is meant by both of these roles. In earlier discussion of the issues that a couple needs to face before marriage, we stated that what two people bring to a marriage is not so important as the degree to which they are able and willing to grow and change together. This point can be extended to apply equally to family living. It is not so much what parents say and do for their children that is important. Rather, what counts is whether they introduce their offspring to an attitude of open and honest struggling for the possibility of constructive living together, even if this demands the overcoming of fears and the sacrificing of hopes.

Parents who try to determine the destiny of their children are as mistaken as those who permissively "understand" their children to death by providing no structure or guidance. The main thing that parents can do for their children, and must do if they want to be responsible parents, is to ready them for an honest coping with problems by manifesting the willingness to do so themselves. In the freedom and warmth of parents' attitudes toward each other, the growing child sees a possible way of living together which he anticipates for himself later. To the degree that parents are unable to exhibit gentleness and responsiveness they wreak havoc on their children's development. Children who are deprived of the experience of growing up in an atmosphere which gives room to realistic self-expression, who are denied parents possessing mutual self-respect—these are the ones who should concern us. Overly eager to seek what they sense is lacking in the home, they plunge into affairs for which they are especially ill prepared.

Often parents assume that they can prevent their children

from being prematurely interested in sex, not to speak of playing around with it, if they carefully avoid both mentioning sex at home and displaying affection which could be interpreted as suggestive of sexual interest. Nothing could be farther from the truth. Parents are not very helpful if the only thing they can do is teach children how to avoid the reality of sex. All they really accomplish in taking this tack is to force the young to go elsewhere for knowledge of and initiation into sex. It is not always prudery that prevents parents from being open and useful to their children in this area. Regrettable as it may be, many parents are themselves confused or even bitter about sex.

We are often told that the concerned parent is one who is in constant and unrestricted communication with his child and that he shows his parental qualifications by his ability to talk freely and factually about sex. If sex could be treated on the same level as learning to brush one's teeth, it might be possible for the parent to be an adequate impersonal trainer for his children. But since sex is indicative of far more, especially of the character of the parent-child relationship, it is asking too much to expect parents to be objective about a relationship in which they are so subjectively involved and have so much at stake. The parent who thinks he must be the complete confidant of his child may actually be lacking in respect for the child's indispensable independence. How much the parent depends for self-esteem on his living up to a parental ideal and so producing the perfect child comes out in his temptation to interfere with the independent growth of his offspring.

Parents whose own relationship manifests respectful curiosity provide their offspring with the setting most conducive to abetting the latter's eagerness to grow and mature. If children sense that parents are willing and able to face any issues, free of the know-it-all attitude or defensiveness, they will welcome the opportunity to share with their parents what bothers and entices them. The family that is filled with such a spirit is free from the chief obstacle in the path of learning to live together.

A good test of whether a family lives in terms of a power struggle or in an attitude of learning together what renders life meaningful is how freely they can discuss sex together. Can the young ones come home and disclose their questions, hopes, and fears about sex to their mother and father? Can parents freely accept what sex looks like to their young, without rushing in and imposing their adult expectations? Can parents and young people reason together, fully recognizing that their respective understandings are limited and not wholly adequate to the others' circumstances? To do this implies that parents are willing to disclose how they have struggled with sex and the conclusions they have reached, knowing well that they may thus reveal their fears, biases, and limitations. If parents and young people misunderstand their love for one another as the parents' willingness to bail the young out of a tight spot and the children's feeling free to bank on this, far from helping each other to grow they only compound their mutual confusion.

The cleavage between the parental and the filial attitude toward the sex play of young people stems from their respective appreciation of the complexities involved in intimate living together. Because of their painful awareness of the obligations, hazards, and tensions associated with starting a family, parents are quick to express their apprehension and disfavor over adolescents' eagerness to experiment with sex. Since these problems have a way of interfering with married sexual pleasures, parents scarcely believe that children are ready to assume the burdens which inevitably are associated with sex. Giving their young timely warning concerning the hard realities of living is admirable, but one wonders sometimes whether it is not the parents' disappointment in their own sexual life which makes them so adamant in their opposition to premarital sex.

PARTNERSHIP AFTER CHILDREARING

If parents live only for their children, what happens after they have left to start their own families? We have seen how difficult it is for parents to encourage their maturing children to seek independence, especially when the way of life chosen by the young shatters secret or admitted parental hopes. Many a parent, frustrated in his own life and marriage, declares proudly that all he lives for is his children. They will do better than he was able to do and fulfill the ambitions he himself never succeeded in realizing.

But suppose the children leave home and ignore their parents' expectations or vicarious daydreaming—what then? Paradoxical as it seems, the success of marital incorporation of sex proves itself after sex has lost its initial fascination and has fulfilled its function of assuring procreation. We have said before that sex is not an end in itself but a means to express living together; this holds unquestionably true for a couple which finds itself childless again.

The art of living and growing together depends on a couple's finding a common ground on which they can meet unreservedly and from which they can evaluate what faces them. The gradual change which marks growing together is that of moving away from mutual dependence on external resources and circumstances, through the phase of their combined involvement in raising and educating children, to the stage of relying on their commonly shared life. From spouse, through parent, to partner, describes the movement of growing together as man and wife.

Each spouse in his respective involvement in the world is bound to be tempted, challenged, frustrated, and enriched. Sexual dialogue registers sensitively, though not with rational clarity, the vibrations of their life experiences. If sex is severed from the rest of a couple's life experience, it degenerates into a repetitive, stagnating routine which fulfills no significant function except the satisfaction of the sexual urge. If sex is not incorporated into the couple's total life awareness, it ceases to play its essential role and loses its significance. That so many middle-aged couples having no apparent marital or other difficulties discontinue having sex together, an experience which was once so enjoyable but has now become a nonsensical chore, suggests that sexual pleasure is not always self-promoting. If a man and wife are unable to express sexually the joys and sorrows of their daily life, they are sure to wander in their fantasies in search of one who will bring back what has been lost. Instead of being so startled when we learn that a nice married friend is having an affair, we should remind ourselves of both the potency and the delicacy of marital sex.

As the advent of children necessitates an adjustment to parenthood and family life on the part of the spouses, with implications for their life as sexual partners, so there is a new stage when children grow up and leave home. This third stage in the process of shared living centers in the change from being primarily parents to being companions. Concern for those who have completed their parental tasks has revolved almost entirely around the profound physical and psychological changes which a woman undergoes in menopause. Today greater life expectancy introduces additional problems.

The attitude that sex is for the young and is outgrown as one matures only reveals a much too narrow understanding of sex. The compelling need to relieve glandular pressure wanes as one grows older, while the susceptibility to environmental stimuli remains. As with many other aspects of human life, later life reveals to what degree a person has learned to broaden the significance of his sexual experience so as to incorporate it constructively into his total life-awareness. If sex has been limited to a momentary relief or a demonstration of one's attractiveness and irresistibility, the older person has nothing left but to look back with nostalgia and, perhaps, regret.

Later life challenges people to enjoy each other in no less amorous fashion than previously, although they may express it in sexual intercourse with decreasing frequency. The relative ease of older people in their attitude toward sex manifests itself usually in their understanding and appreciation of young people's coping with sex and sexuality. It may well be that some grandparents are more easily accepted as confidants and better able to guide adolescents in sexual matters than some parents. Not so intimately connected with and less anxious about the lives of the young than parents, older people can frequently offer objectivity and wisdom concerning sex. Distance from the immediacy of direct involvement makes possible the precious gift of humor, thus giving the questions and problems of sex a new perspective.

To be of such service to the young presupposes that older people have not only reflected on their own sexual experience but learned from so doing that one can never apply his own views as the measure of what the young should and should not do. Being well aware that change is the very fabric of life, grandparents can also assist their own children in recognizing that each generation must rebel and find its own way.

The significance which sex can carry for older people is much greater than what derives from their role as counselor to those younger. Having grown through adjusting to each other as spouses and struggling together as parents, they can now let their intimate and loving knowledge of each other ripen into enjoyment of life together as it now is. Familiarity does not always breed contempt.

To be able to exhibit such delight more than makes up for the pain and difficulties which have been encountered on the way. If sex is the indicator that not only one person's life is becoming integrated within itself but two people's existence is fused into a unit, then sex finds its consummation in the couple's unending pleasure in each other. This joy enriches all whom they encounter.

## DISRUPTIONS IN THE INCORPORATION OF MARITAL SEXUALITY

The significance of the phases in the sexual relationship of two partners—engagement, marriage before children are born, parenthood, and marriage after children have left home—can be highlighted by considering the disruptive forces which threaten the relationship. Three of these difficulties, infidelity, divorce, and death of a spouse, offer us the unpleasant occasion to ask ourselves not only what has been lost but, more important, why it did not work out much better. But we can gain from former experiences only if we are willing to face as honestly as possible our original attitude and approach to marriage and family.

It is hoped that the following will lead neither to unrealistic lamentations nor to self-accusations, both of which enslave one to a helpless rehashing of the past. Learning from the past comes only to the person who is willing to change and who begins today to face the future more wisely.

### INFIDELITY

Religious and social moralism, in black-and-white distinction between good and bad, declares that infidelity is wrong. When legally labeled as adultery, infidelity is sufficient reason for divorce. Our moralistic attitude toward infidelity is a good example of our tendency to judge effects and forget the cause. Moralists still operate under the naïve assumption that declaring something wrong will stop people from doing it. The result, however, is merely that people try to enjoy the forbidden fruit without getting caught.

Faithfulness represents the fruit of one's willingness to allow an intimate and constant relationship to re-form one's attitude. Faithfulness stems from and depends on a basic change in outlook toward oneself and the other. Infidelity signals that sexuality either never has been incorporated into marital sex or has been allowed to disengage itself again into a self-centered lusting. Lust is a symptom of unincorporated sexuality. As long as one expects fulfilling satisfaction to come from an external source, he will keep lusting. Infidelity consists in allowing the object of lust to reshape one's sense of value. Both fidelity and infidelity center in an agent which determines a sense of value. Fidelity's agent is the shared experience of marriage. Infidelity's agent is the imagined or real satisfaction of an extramarital relationship.

If the unfaithful blames his marriage and his spouse for his being prompted to become unfaithful, he is partly correct. But he overlooks the fact that he is a part of this marriage and cannot appraise himself separately from his spouse. He is not an unfortunate victim but a deserter. He has forsaken his marital identity and substituted for it the assumed identity of the single person.

The real issue in the problem of infidelity remains at the level of expectations. What is expected, consciously or unconsciously, determines attitude toward marriage and vulnerability to extramarital temptations. If we want to attack the root of the infidelity problem, we must understand the psychological role of expectations. They link our urge to expand and enrich ourselves with an external opportunity which seems to promise help in activating the urge.

Expectations are necessarily vague and tentative as they bring together an unclear image of what is desired and an untested appraisal of the external opportunity. We want most of all, we assume, to be happier, more satisfied, and thereby better able to realize our potentials. We also believe that opportunities around us will offer exactly what was missing in the past. Tantalizing uncertainty moves back and forth between "maybe" and "maybe not," reinforcing self-accusations of not daring to take a chance when it presents itself and self-addressed warnings that we may gamble frivolously at stakes too high for our circumstances.

The emotional torment involved in expectations consists in awareness that on both sides of the coin there is a true rendition of ourselves. We have not yet fully realized the potentials we sense are ours; on the other hand, following our expectations may mean a jump from the frying pan into the open fire. Expectations do not yield factual certainty until they are tried out. The hesitantly wavering person is therefore easy prey to the accidental lure of the moment and the nudging whim of temptation.

The sexual interpretation of how expectations work demands little imagination. The spouse stubbornly tries to quiet down the inner nagging that he is not fulfilled sexually in his marriage and truly deserves a better treatment than he is receiving from his mate. Trying to be faithful and pleasant at home, he has never mentioned his dissatisfaction to anybody, least of all to his spouse. All it takes to set his secret yearning aflame is an encounter with the person who is "just what he always wanted." Tipping the balance may well be an innocent encouragement from a person who appears so tempting and circumstances which seem to cooperate in providing an almost secure and ideal setting. He may argue that he was married on the basis of a mistaken self-knowledge; now that his eyes have been opened to the "real" self everything will be different and better. This enticing argument for viewing infidelity in a positive light as the first step in the right direction obscures the hard fact that two wrongs do not make a right. Leaping over a past mistake does not free us from the guilt of not having come to terms with the past.

The only effective antidote to tempting expectation is to convert the soil on which it grows into the ground on which actual personhood is affirmed and enriched. The temptation to infidelity starves when a marital relation unfolds and blossoms. When two mates can nakedly enjoy each other there is little inducement to sneak out in fantasy or reality to the supposedly greener pasture of infidelity.

We must ask ourselves, as honestly and radically as we can,

how it is possible to live in marriage realistically without becoming unfaithful. The high rate of promiscuity and spouse swapping at weekend parties demands forthright interpretation. How much does our style of life, with its high expectations, succeed not only in dictating our way of living but in rendering us unable to maintain intact the traditional institutions of marriage and the family?

If husband and wife, unreservedly and without pretense, keep sharing their mutual and their respective doubts, questions, fears, and especially their wishful expectations, they have thereby found a solid basis for a common life. If both spouses come to each other sexually to celebrate their unswerving determination to remain human and do so first of all for each other and together, they have unwrapped the secret of ever renewed sex pleasure.

## DIVORCE

Divorce terminates one out of four American marriages today and we still squabble about the circumstances under which legally to grant divorce. We cling to the fading hope that human failure and social decay can be legislated out of existence. The only thing that actually terminates the usefulness of a marriage and symbolizes its destructiveness is that two people cannot tolerate living together. The degree of oppressiveness of the living together and the amount of destructiveness which their marriage produces should be the measure for deciding whether the spouses are to be allowed to go their separate ways.

Divorce poses the legal and social problem of what constitutes marriage, what designates its actuality, and what terminates its social legitimacy and acceptability. How can society, and by what authority, decide about a human contract which is so highly intimate and differs in character from one case to the next? Every society has an immense interest in the health and stability of its marriages. Legally, a society can impose rules and regulations on its institutions, but it cannot infuse them with health and endurance.

Divorce indicates the point at which the cost of preserving marriage appears too high. Regardless of the legal statute or social label under which divorce may be granted, in human terms it indicates that the marital partners believe they can no longer live together. Divorce represents the final recognition of two married people, perhaps more strongly felt by one spouse, that further living together could only result in mutual destruction.

The phraseology of one partner's "divorcing" the other is misleading. It points out only who first filed divorce papers with the court. In reality, neither divorces the other; the court officially acknowledges that a marriage is broken beyond reasonable hope of repair. It is not merely the institution of marriage that breaks down; the two partners are broken in the process as well.

That in a divorce one leaves marital experience as a broken person is unfortunate, but not always detrimental. Depending on how one entered and maintained marriage, it may well be that one needed to be broken down. If selfish expectations were high and willingness to cooperate low, there was no other possibility but the breakdown of the marriage.

In a profound sense, the new attitude that a divorced person gains from the painful experience of brokenness is the attitude needed for any form of intimate living together. Had he been willing to forsake some of his stubbornly held principles during marriage, divorce might never have become necessary. Remarriage, after divorce, should therefore be weighed in the light of how deep and realistic the learning experience of the divorced has been. If he justifies his right to be married again by pointing out how terribly he was wronged by his first mate, one can well foresee that he is probably headed for a repeat performance of his first disaster.

American society still cannot be said to have freed itself of the stigma inherited from the traditional religious and social taboos against divorce. Evidence that divorce continues to be regarded as a blot on one's character is easily cited. Witness what happens when a divorced person seeks political office. Spouses acknowledge their adherence to these taboos when they agree to continue to live together under the same roof "for the sake of the children," though mutual respect and concern have died. This viewpoint takes little into account that spouses who continue to live together on such a basis may thus more severely emotionally damage and confuse their children than if they were to make a clean break.

Treating divorce as an easy exit from a marriage arrangement regarded as tentative from the start equally misses the point of what is involved in divorce. However inevitable, divorce always represents a failure which has to be faced up to if one is to grow from the experience. In the process of divorce, two people who had been united in a relationship of intimate sharing lose their commonality, slide into individual isolations, and may begin sniping at each other. Regardless of each partner's estimate of his respective gains and losses, it is a miscalculation to ignore the past impact of living together as husband and wife. Even though they may work out a relatively amicable settlement and part as friends, it is impossible for either to pick up the pieces and go on living as if he or she had not been wed to the other. Each carries away the visible imprints of the life that once was shared.

To the degree that an ex-spouse does not come to terms with his failure, he is certain to carry with him the shadow of unacknowledged fear and undue expectation that may well poison any future attempts to establish a happy marriage. Even those who have done their best to work through their guilt and shortcomings face real difficulties in adjusting from one marriage relationship to another. Not only is there the constant temptation to compare the present spouse with the former, who is now seen in the milder light of hindsight, but it is easy to slide into expecting the present spouse to be all that the former was not.

That children are involved in most divorces adds to the problem of adjustment. How children see and are affected by the divorce and remarriage of their parents can hardly be fully appreciated by any adult, let alone the parents. Caught in their divided loyalties, children have to cross the no-man's-land between feuding parents. The confusion and wrenching experienced by the children are aggravated when they are treated as pawns by the parents.

In a sense, divorce is only the last link in a series of breaks in the marriage relationship, but with the significant difference that it precludes any easy reconciliation. Marriage involves the partners in a process of drawing together and apart. The mere fact that during the week the husband leaves for work while his wife devotes herself to her duties in the home and community means a separation making it necessary for the partners to find each other again. And this is but one small example of the constant moving apart and together of marriage. In their respective contacts the spouses are influenced by a variety of suggestions and values which need to be aired and sorted out when they come together again. A good deal of flexibility is needed by both so that each will have room to introduce new possibilities into their common living. If their marriage is to come to terms with the new and the different, they must together evaluate it and out of their evaluation decide what they will incorporate and what they will reject. Crucial in their struggle with change in marriage is that their *common* life be decisive. When a couple can no longer arrive at a genuine consensus in which the will of each is absorbed into their common aim, the marriage is in danger of dissolving.

From an appreciation of the unavoidable trauma represented by divorce we can see more realistically what is required to render marriage an operative, growing experience. That two people learn to give each other room to unfold and change, while not losing sight of and respect for each other, is probably the single most important ingredient in a successful marriage. Comparable to the body's two distinct but inseparable movements of breathing in and out, a marriage relationship is sustained by the freedom to enjoy closeness but also the ability to tolerate distance. It is important that husband and wife not assume that they know all about each other and so take each other for granted. Often the lure of an extramarital affair stems from the seductive possibility that another will see us in a new light and, by not crowding us, allow us to be different.

## DEATH OF A SPOUSE

Death, inescapable and final, reminds us that we can neither take our own life for granted nor count on living together interminably. The death of a spouse separates a union of life, leaving one wounded mate behind. Were we to ask for a proof that marriage is more than merely a casual, tentative agreement, we need only remember the partner who, after the death of a spouse, must build another life.

At first glance, the most striking experience of the widowed is that the rupture seems almost unreal; every effort to accept and build again appears to be an act of unfaithfulness to the deceased. This difference only appears so cruelly striking because the circumstances have changed while the bereaved has not. Easily a victim of routine, the human is slow to change or to adapt himself to a new situation. Lonely and lost, he finds it difficult to activate those resources which would allow him to go on without his spouse. Unconsciously he may resent being deserted.

How is the widowed to find a way between loyalty to the past marriage and awareness that a new chapter in life must begin? One can neither deny the past nor sacrifice the present and what is yet to be. Almost like the adolescent leaving home for the first time, the widowed must ask himself anew: Who am I and how can I order my life?

Avoiding the real challenge of a spouse's death, current funeral practices go out of their way to deny the finality of the dead's departure. From beautifying the corpse so that it looks like a comfortably resting human to references to a reunion in heaven, they do their best to ignore what is, as far as we know, the dead end of human life. There seems to be a terrible difficulty in accepting death's closure, unpredictable and unavoidable as it is, as a reality which cannot be appealed.

Probably, death is so intolerable when it strikes in our midst because we do such a good job of banning its presence from our awareness. Far from preparing for the challenge of death, we escape as much as we can any possible reminder of its possibility. Yet there is a real question of which is more morbid: to face death for what it is and live accordingly, or to live as if we never would have to face death and then to be shocked at its occurrence.

The truly shocking aspect of death consists in its forcing us, both the dying and the surviving, to let go, to give up, to face uncertainty over which we have no control. The threat of death reveals at once what our basic attitude toward life is. Maybe we should learn to live so we can accept death rather than to die with a nagging suspicion that we never really have lived. The reality of death questions our way of living; our earthly beliefs and achievements do not, as we often religiously put it, alleviate our having to die.

Actually, we could learn from biology that death and renewal are constant happenings in our body tissue and chemistry. At every moment some cells cease to exist. At the same time, new cells are born and take over from the decaying ones. The abrupt change that final death symbolizes is only the most obvious demonstration of what life represents, namely, the experience of constant change.

Above all else, death makes us strikingly aware of what is always involved, though usually ignored, in a marital relationship. When one marries, he must die to the independent life of the single person. When children are born, a couple must die to their exclusive twosomeness. When children grow up and leave home, parents have to die to their claim to authority and control. Apart from these major events entailing death, there are the innumerable changes and transitions encountered in daily living which are experienced as death to the old and openness to the new. In short, dying is very much a part of living and refers to an experience far wider than that with which we usually identify the term.

As can be gathered from the foregoing discussion of three threats to the incorporation of sex in marriage—infidelity, divorce, and death of a spouse—marriage is anything but an easy relation. The difficulty is that marital success does not so much depend on what we do or don't do; fulfillment or failure in marriage depends on what we are and how well we communicate this to each other. As its Latin roots convey, "communication" means literally to bring together.

In marriage we bring to each other what we are. What both partners are is their common ground and possession. To withdraw from this common ground and try to single out what each one owes is to break the marriage, whether the attempt is willful or, as in case of death, accidental. One could call such withdrawal sin. Before the term *sin* became moralistically mangled, it suggested separation of that which should not be separated. When in marriage one or both partners withdraw, there results more than empty space between them. Such a vacuum is actually filled with images, experiences, fears, and most of all projections of one's own guilt into accusations toward the other.

Neither sexuality nor sex can endure this separation. Sexuality drives us into naked intimacy with another. And sex is the celebration of the intimacy in which each partner receives his fulfillment from the other. In infidelity, sexuality can no longer penetrate to the partner or receive him for what he is. Hence it becomes redirected to another person. In divorce, the possibility of sex is eliminated. But this is symbolic of a far more profound elimination. The two spouses have no more common ground or possession. They have severed what they were and had in common. In death, final separation, although not of one's own making, brings demonstratively into the open how little there is left if one is thrown upon oneself again and how important it is to rebuild a new life of incorporation.

# CHAPTER V

# LEARNING TO LIVE SEXUALLY

LEARNING TO LIVE is a task which faces every generation anew. At times the challenge may be to learn to live with or against external restrictions and encroachments on personal liberty. At other times, it is not to lose ourselves in too many and competing opportunities. One generation or culture suffers from an inability to understand and enjoy the world because its religion insists that visible reality is an illusion, vastly inferior to the "real" life yet to come. Others are so overwhelmed with their actual state of affairs that they lack any sense of vision and purpose. Since the day-to-day dealing with the immediate situation absorbs all their energy and attention, they do not know how to look beyond it. Learning to live demands that we recognize the tensions we live in, see them for what they are, and through their interaction in human consciousness let a more confident understanding arise of what man's place and function in the world shall be.

The phrase *learning to live sexually* must be taken quite literally. Learning to come to terms with our sexuality is only one, though an essential, part of the attempt to find and orient ourselves. Living sexually implies living as sexual beings, neither fighting against the evil lust of the flesh nor replacing full-fledged human living with an exclusive and escapist indulgence in sexual orgies. Crucial here is the need to recognize that we live to discover life, not to prove or disprove some religious, social, or moral presupposition. We are not on earth to live up to any preconceived ideal or idol or to be judged and beaten down by a fictitious philosophy or doctrine of man and life. We are alive here to grow and mature by grasping and unfolding the potentials for human development.

Such writers as Kafka, Dostoievski, Ibsen, O'Neill, among many others, have depicted how the tensions man lives with can either destroy him or catapult him into true greatness. Paraphrasing the central theme of the Greek tragedies, these artists underscore the two main options which man finds before him. Either way he turns he cannot escape his guilt; this dilemma is the original sense of the word *tragic*. If he forsakes his potentials for finding his own way, he is guilty of not furthering through his life experience the ongoing growth of mankind. If he follows the urge to discover new and promising ways of life, he is guilty of separating himself from the corporate life of those who fear any disruption of their usual mode of living.

The challenge, therefore, lies in learning to live in tension without prematurely resolving it. People must fight the desire to identify quickly with either pole of the tension because it is precisely out of the endured tension that new solutions and promises arise. The prime example of having to live in tension and possibly benefiting from it is our existence as sexual creatures in need of finding the way toward sexual confidence. It may thus be helpful to consider three areas of tension and ask ourselves how living in these could lead to incorporating sex and integrating life-awareness.

## IMAGINATION VERSUS FANTASY

Everyday parlance seldom distinguishes between fantasy and imagination. We mean about the same thing when we say that somebody has a wild fantasy or a wild imagination, that he imagines things or that things live only in his fantasy. Yet there is a distinct difference between the origin and function of fantasies and the power and range of imagination. Actually, the two stay in tension with each other, although they cannot be neatly sorted out from their intermingling. Fantasy without imagination remains dim. Imagination without fantasy lacks emotional color and vibrance.

As Freudian psychoanalysis has taught us, fantasies emerge out of the personal unconscious. And, as Jung has added with fascinating suggestiveness but less dependable clinical evidence, the possibility that the personal unconscious is open to a deeper and wider collective, cultural unconscious should not be ruled out. We should not force a reduction of our fantasies to mere experiences which have not yet been fully digested. Fantasies arise whenever, in day or night dreams, our rational censor allows us to float without the restrictions of time and space. Fantasies, whether pleasant or disturbing, free us for the moment from the bondage of our given life situation.

What is especially important here is that fantasies both bespeak unconscious leanings and challenge rational assumptions and moral principles. Fantasies tell us that we are not exactly what we rationally think we are and morally would like to be. Thus they call in question our arrangements and oversimplifications. In their upward surge for recognition, however, fantasies clash with the imagination.

At the opposite pole from fantasizing, imagination stems from the realm of the conscious mind and reaches down into the unconscious, into the area of the possible-but-not-yet-realized. We are not dreaming but rather playing with possibilities when we imagine. Taking off from what we know, we explore what could be and how it might be if a given fact or circumstance were different. Imagination is hence decisive in artistic creativity as well as in scientific hypothesizing.

Imagination liberates the intellect from constantly having to limit itself to the analysis of what is already at hand. Imagination entertains the possibility of change, even of radical break and contrast. In this questioning and loosening of the intellect, imagination meets fantasy. Fantasy brings to imagination the emotional charge of desire or fear while imagination adds to fantasy the conceptual clarification of what actually could be and how it possibly would be. In their respective aims lies their inevitable clash.

These abstract definitions become at once more concrete when we turn to the specific interest of this book, the sexual significance of fantasy and imagination. Sexual fantasies are fed by a profound desire for unity. No man forgets altogether in his unconscious that at birth he stepped out of the womb, out of the protecting and nourishing unity of mother and child. No adult ever fully gets over the process of having to leave, step by step, the protective unity of childhood, home, peer group, or school to enter a world he can never fully trust. Individuation spells separation and inner loneliness. Sexual fantasies keep the dim memories of a "paradise lost" alive and urge us to seek a new unity. Since, short of neurotic or even psychotic regression, there is no way back to the womb, sexual fantasies prompt us to look for a new union based on what we have come to call the *self*.

The sexual character of our fantasies emphasizes the tension between what of ourselves we want to unfold and confirm out and what we desire to come to us as our complement. Their drive points both outward and inward. We want to discover and prove ourselves by becoming one with the other and, at the same time, draw the other into ourselves so as to gain enrichment and confirmation. We should, therefore, learn to interpret our sexual fantasies beyond the crude, paramount evidence of the instinctual, glandular drives. Fantasies teach us something about ourselves. They—especially the sexual ones—teach us how much we actually have left infantile unity with the parental home, how we unconsciously feel about ourselves, and how we hope to achieve a new, adult, independent selfhood.

Especially because fantasies are less encumbered by our rational censor than are thoughts, they can indicate more truthfully who we really are and where in fact we stand in our personal development. Sexual fantasies should not be taken as nothing but the secret ticker tape of the lonely man in his privacy. We may not feel like broadcasting our fantasies abroad, but that should not mislead us into regarding them as nothing but a meager substitute for living and interacting with others. It is indeed a genuine mark of true union between lovers when they dare to tell each other their respective fantasies. This intimacy goes beyond even the physical nakedness of sex.

The same view holds true for imagination. Shared imagination is better than an isolated single one. Since imagination represents the reach of the conscious mind into the realm of the unconscious, such sharing is all the more important. Otherwise, the individual's attempt to realize his own fantasies is hampered by and limited exclusively to his attitude toward himself. We are all too ready to separate the sheep from the goats among our fantasies. We may play with, but then quickly suppress, those which threaten us either by their libertinism or their challenge to our self-image. But if we share our imagination with a loved one we not only dare to face our naked self but can begin to ask how it could be realized in actual life. This is the function of imagination. It entertains and probes ways and means of feeding fantasies into the conscious attitude toward life. Awareness of our selves and our lives is thereby enriched, and fantasies are lifted into a constructive function. Those fantasies which are not integrated into consciousness sink back into the unconscious and fester.

Imagination thus serves as a vital link between the world of conscious thought and the underworld of unacknowledged fantasy. Itself identified with neither, imagination introduces to the conscious mind the possible which has arisen out of the fleeting imagery of fantasies. Unclear moods and tempers can crystallize around imagined concepts thrown into the pool of vague feelings. Likewise, imagination instills cold rational thought with the warmth and pulse of feeling.

The exchange character of imagination can best be illustrated by listening to casual usage of the verbs *to think* and *to imagine*. When a child asks whether there are people on the moon, one answers, "I don't think so." If someone asks whether the inhabitants of the earth could survive on the moon, we respond in the light of recent space exploration with, "I imagine so." The degree of verified or not yet verified probability makes the difference between thinking and imagining something.

### SENSE

We *imagine* what probably could be, while we *know* what is. Imagination mediates between a fantasy which probably could be realized and an assumed knowledge which easily could be challenged. Out of the exposure of thought and fantasy to each other, imagination produces what we call *sense*. The double meaning of sense must here be maintained. We intuitively sense something before we can be sure whether it will be affirmed or denied. The other meaning of sense implies an awareness of reality which stands between fantasy and information.

Only the dimension suggested when we speak of "common sense," or, in more colloquial fashion, "horse sense," needs to be added to indicate the total range of significance of the word *sense*. We are "making sense" when our utterance or action conveys being in tune with what is generally understood as positive and constructive. The dimension of sense reveals, therefore, not only that man is individually in need of integrating feeling and thought into one whole personality, but also that he depends on being integrated into a wider social collective. In this light it can be appreciated how much sex and sense are intertwined.

The brunt of the argument here is that we have to overcome the false and detrimental split between a view of the senses as powerful and possibly destructive forces and a view of rational intellect as an always cool, factual, objective control. The senses and the power of reasoning are constantly interacting positively through what we call *sense*. This interaction is not a power struggle in which the instincts blindly demand the fullest possible range of freedom while reason restricts them because of societal norms and taboos. Common sense consists of the realization that, as sexual beings, we live within and depend upon a social structure. But we cannot merely agree with and adjust to the social rules and customs around us. They, in turn, depend on our ongoing re-evaluation of their functional worth. Society is made up of us, the people, who try to find our way. Society does not rule by eternal decrees and wield absolute power; it can be bent to the will of its constituents. Likewise, our senses need to be recognized and channeled into creative expression. Only when we try to deny or hold them down do they degenerate into the dumb, beastly forces of our fearful caricatures of them.

"Common sense" is a collective, not an individualistic, term. All of us are incorporated into the tapestry of common living, not merely on the rational or the instinctual level, but where both elements, through imagination, meet and cooperate. We sense our place and function within the social structure as we also sense whether this structure allows us to live honestly and decently. In spite of all our talk about liberty it should not be taken for granted that we know how to live or that our present way of life unquestionably affords us the opportunity to unfold our best individual and corporate potentials. Our young ones sense strongly that we must apply the whole force of imagination in order to come to terms with ourselves as sexual beings and with our society as a potentially meaningful body of interacting people.

## SELF-AWARENESS AND IDENTITY

What the process of coming to terms with ourselves as individuals and as members of society demands of us is best illustrated by the interplay between self-awareness and identity. The single unique characteristic which distinguishes man from the rest of creation is his ability to be aware of himself. It follows that the more clearly we are aware of ourselves, the more human we are, and the better prepared to come up with a flexible way of living together which can make sense.

Under the immense impact of the social and behavioral sciences we have made great strides toward knowing ourselves better. We have mitigated the rigidity of religious and social moralism while beginning to shoulder some of the responsibilities of living together. Human interaction entails more than merely giving each one his due while leaving the field wide open for a competitive free-for-all in which everyone is for himself. Still, we are but on the threshold of envisaging that human growth is tantamount to and dependent on the unending development of self-awareness. Barely do we reach one level of becoming aware of ourselves before we must amend our knowledge in order to grapple with the understanding of what the next phase in life will present and demand of us.

Identity represents the fruit of our having integrated some of the diverse aspects of personality at one stage of the process of growing in self-awareness. We reach a degree of identity whenever what we know of ourselves as individual persons coincides with what we appear to be in the eyes of others. Identity, therefore, brings together self-awareness with self-expression and its acceptance by others. Identity neither springs exclusively out of self-appraisal nor is solely the label by which the environment characterizes us. Indeed, these two poles of identity are always in tension; neither is able to dispense with the other. Increasing self-awareness will constantly break open and amend a specific identity we have achieved. By the same token, our status in society will tend to freeze us in the specific functional identity that we have reached. Nevertheless, growing self-awareness orients itself toward the images of what we have been, are now, and can become to others. Also, our place and function as active members of a social structure can only be maintained as long as our self-knowledge allows us to conform to our social image.

The tension between self-awareness and identity plays an especially crucial role in sex. We cannot be confident and self-giving in sex before we are at ease with ourselves as we have become aware of ourselves. But society assigns us a specific role and behavior through which to express and share our sexuality. Self-image and social image may be miles apart, leaving us in the no-man's-land between. A young person, but not he alone, may especially not be sexually at ease and free within the socially prescribed frame of conduct for the "boy and girl game." Regardless of whether a person thinks of himself as a good citizen, a Don Juan, a rebel, or a nobody, he must find ways confidently to express himself either through or in spite of the image, simply because sex is an interpersonal affair. Many a person may in public play nearly to perfection the role of one or another social image. But this does not mean that in the privacy of his intimate sex life he can uphold the image of his public appearance. If he cannot do so, he fails to have any dependable identity and falls between his private and public life. Out of this tension arises, therefore, a more fundamental tension between meaning and action.

After the child learns to say "No" and discovers that his "No" leads to certain consequences, he has to deal with the problem of meaning and action. Often we hear ourselves say that we did not really mean what we said. Or we acknowledge ruefully that, had we only known beforehand what our action would mean to others, we certainly would not have done what we did. Meaning and action, obviously, do not always go together. Good intention does not automatically lead to positive action, and actions sometimes becloud the original meaning which prompted them. To bring meaning and action into conformity requires careful effort. We must be sure that we know what we mean and are selective in the ways we translate meaning into action.

But meaning itself is not a single, homogeneous entity. What I mean to myself may be quite different from what I mean to others. What I mean to be, and how I intend to become what I mean to be, can be markedly out of tune with each other. The same holds true for actions. An action can be a most honest execution of a decision arrived at independently and with my best judgment. The same action can represent a merely mechanical reaction to external prompting without my realizing what I am doing or what it means.

Experience with sex can certainly bear out and illustrate what has just been said. Whenever lovers feel free enough to talk about and review their sex life, their conversations invariably center around the discrepancy between meaning and action. To his dismay, each partner can even discover that it is difficult to know what he himself means and even more demanding to anticipate what his action may mean to the other. Yet only through such attempts can the love life of two sexual partners be safeguarded against the danger of meaningless action and routine. As is well known, marital difficulties and extramarital escapades often stem from marital sex life's having lost its significance as a bridge between two people.


## INSIGHT

Most baffling in sexual difficulties is the fact that we obviously mean well and even act to the best of our knowledge but still are sometimes unable to get at the roots of the predicament. What is missing is *insight*. Literally, insight implies the human ability to see into the dynamics of the interplay between meaning and action. Insight is the middle ground from which meaning can be illuminated and action guided. Meaning constitutes the personal significance that factual objects assume for us through experience. It is easy to say, like Gertrude Stein, that an apple is an apple is an apple. In other words, one is tempted to believe that an object retains without wavering its factual significance for everyone at all times and everywhere. But for him who actually encounters it, the object can assume vastly different significance from what it had for an uninvolved observer. An apple means something quite different to the child who eats it from what it means to the government economist who sees it as an agricultural product.

Insight relates partial significance to total meaning. Insight sensitizes us to the context in which a person, thing, or event assumes its particular significance. Insight, therefore, is the vehicle which helps us to gain a better understanding of ourselves, to weigh the influences that affect us, and to appraise our actions accordingly. However, insight is not merely a momentary flash, which like fantasy captivates us briefly only to dissipate as quickly.

Through memory we store essential insights, remembering not only what has actually happened but what it meant to us and how we responded to it.

The remark above that self-awareness distinguishes man from all other creatures laid the groundwork for saying that such awareness grows with the sum total of insights. Remembered insights permit reflection. Like a reflector, past experiences constitute a bright background on which every new experience, insight, or action bounces with special intensity. Through insight we perceive continuity in what we are and appreciate why we act the way we do. Without insight we could know neither ourselves nor others; we could not evaluate the significance of human action.

It is no accident that psychoanalysis relates sex and insight. As a prime personal act between two people sex requires, more than any other human activity or experience, the light of insight. The degree of insight within and between people sexually involved regulates the mixture of sexual expression and sexual activity.

## EXPRESSION VERSUS ACTIVITY

Sexual activities do not necessarily represent a person's full self-disclosure. One can "have" sex or "make" love without expressing himself or being fully involved. Nor is it only in the act of sexual intercourse that sexual expression takes place. Since we are sexual creatures, our whole manner of communicating is influenced by what we are. But only insofar as, through insight, we have become aware of ourselves do we know how to correlate sexual expression and activity. We can willfully express the self only as we have become aware of it. Likewise, we can elevate sexual activities to the level of genuine self-expression only to the degree that we appreciate and share the latter more than the former.

Unfortunately, too much of the discussion of sexual behavior focuses on what to do and what not to do, as if sex were something which has to be "handled," as a separate entity. Parents, filled with the traditional fears for their children of premarital pregnancy or venereal diseases, not only ignore the modern preventive pharmaceutical means but fail to convey to their young people that the decisive question is whether the young are mature enough to live sensitively and respectfully for each other in a constructive relationship. If young people can be in this way responsible for each other, sex will no longer be abused as a substitute for living, but will be seen as a shared self-expression. Parents who are wise enough to instill such an attitude in their children will free them from the temptation of using sex as a symbol of rebellious independence from parental advice.

A peculiar characteristic of the American understanding of sex is the tendency to identify sex narrowly with the act of coitus. This stunted view of what is sexual expresses itself in the popular meaning attached to such words as *flirt* and *erotic*. The former is usually employed to describe a sexually suggestive person or behavior. The typical picture which comes to mind when one hears this term is that of a woman eliciting the interest of a man other than her spouse, with the implication that sexual intercourse is to follow. To restrict *flirt* in this way is unfortunate. Originally, flirting constituted the freedom of enjoying and expressing one's sexual confidence in the presence of the other sex, without either suggesting or expecting such playfulness to lead to sexual intercourse. To the contrary, this uninhibited expression of self-contentment and delight was possible only because it was unquestionably assumed that nobody could misunderstand flirting as an invitation to intercourse.

The devaluation of the erotic is similarly unfortunate. At least in America, "erotic" has suffered the same degeneracy as *flirt*. It has become synonymous with the sexual, understood as coitus. When one is told that a person behaves "erotically," the implication is that he manifests a hardly restrained desire to get on with passionate lovemaking. Such usage is a far cry from the meaning given to the word by the Greeks. Springing from the cults of ancient Greek religion, eros represents the intense, sensitive life-awareness which overcomes man, opening him so that he can participate in the dynamics of life. Caught up in the erotic, he perceives the essence of life in everything he encounters, and responds to it intuitively. The erotic state can, therefore, be best likened to what we describe as being in love. Everything looks and feels different and wonderful to the one who is in love.

Thereby enlivened, man senses the all-encompassing order of the cosmos and re-creates it in behavior, in arts, and in social structure. The free man, the truly creative man, is the one who is conscious of such participation and, therefore, can share with his fellows the insight and excitement which his erotic involvement with the world elicits. Eros, thus, far from being limited to one specific segment of human awareness, actually refers to the discovery of life and of having a significant, integral part in it.

## EXPERIENCE VERSUS PRINCIPLES

It has been tradition to frown upon the frivolous heresy that in sex one can and should learn from experience. Only recently have we become more relaxed about married people's improving their sexual skills by consulting guides and manuals. But except for such technical points as how to achieve simultaneous orgasm in the marital bed it has been strictly held that socially acceptable principles should govern sexual behavior. Little thought has been given how such principles originated and how relative they may be to our particular social, economic, and cultural situation.

It has been reported that even our Victorian forebears were not altogether sure about the ban on premarital sex. Although they would not have thought of having their daughters engage in anything as dangerous or vulgar as losing their virginity before the wedding night, well-to-do parents of a bridegroom would send him quietly abroad so that he might learn "something."

In raising doubts on the worth of restricting sex to marriage, this book is not suggesting that the freedom to have sexual relations with anyone one pleases solves anything. The point is, rather, that the principled rejection of premarital sex under any and all circumstances solves nothing either, because it distracts attention from the real issue of what is at stake in living together. By adhering to this principle we refuse to accept the adult responsibility to help young people to see sex in its proper context as the gauge of the ability to live together creatively.

When we insist on the rigid rule of no sex before marriage, we put the whole burden on the uninitiated young to come to terms with an aspect of life which, as our attitude indicates, has not elicited our greatest ease or imagination. It must be clearly stated that learning from experience is very different from wildly promiscuous and mostly senseless indulging in sex for its own sake. Such a chaotic abuse of sex is certainly not more respectful of the person or more helpful than a general principle established with no regard for its consequences to the people it tried to rule. The acid test of whether experience involves the total and responsible man lies in whether it leads him to be willing to reach an appropriate decision.

DECISION

No one who knows the frailty and fallibility of human nature likes to make binding decisions. We all would prefer that situations decide for themselves. *Deciding* entails willingness to put on trial everything we have learned and are aware of and to commit ourselves to suffer the consequences of the decision. The less we know who we are, let alone what we want, the more difficult the deciding. The result of a decision may go far beyond our resources to back it up.

The colloquial complaint of not being able to make up one's mind bespeaks well what is involved in inability to decide. Obviously the "mind," far from being an integrated indicator of what is known, is merely a disoriented conglomeration of impressions and opinions, none of which gains decisive victory over the others. We cannot make up our mind when we sense that the maturity of our judgment is not equal to the magnitude of our decision. We may have many biases and reservations, but we have not yet learned to shape them into a pointed indication. Confronted with the complexity of an actual situation, we suddenly realize that we can no longer depend on the repetition of unscrutinized principles but have to dare to learn from experience and to decide in its light. What we have not tested for ourselves we must indeed accept on faith and hearsay. The question is whether we should attempt decision making on such precarious ground.

In sexual matters decision making is all the more complex because it usually involves at least two, if not more, people. Reaching a decision is thus a mutual affair rather than an arbitrary closure by one. Of course, sexual decision making can be avoided by allowing the upsurge of instinctual and emotional urges to overwhelm any rational reflection. Afterward we can try to pretend that nothing happened or that we were merely the innocent victims of overpowering circumstances far beyond our control. But today most people are psychologically too sophisticated to imitate Adam and Eve behind the bushes.

When people decide together on the nature and course of their sexual relationship, the true quality of their personhood is called to the fore. At this point their readiness is revealed, both to bind themselves and to endure the possible wrench of falling apart again. Most of us are not sure whether we can take the risk of binding ourselves or the jolt of being rejected by the other and thrown back on solitude. The argument for the incorporation of sex is based on its demand for total involvement if sex is to play its distinct role of re-evaluating and affirming our naked humanity. Deciding in sexual matters calls for the ability to face nakedly what we are yet to be.

## VALUES AND MEANING

That we need no longer depend childishly on preordained principles does not imply that there is a virtue in being absolutely unprincipled. The question is rather how our principles emerge and how flexible we are in applying them. Living by principles alone is as impossible as is the attempt to float through life without ever realizing that certain guidelines are bound to emerge from experience if we are honest enough to recognize them for what they are. Our attitude is inescapably influenced by what we have learned in life. There is a difference between blind and wise living: the wise man knows what impinges on his judgment. The issue thus is to realize the motivating forces that affect us and to distinguish between principles that have outlived their immediate relevance and principles that retain the essence of what we conceive to be the indispensable meaning of life. In horse-and-buggy days one might have been well served by a principle of never riding in a carriage drawn by overexcited horses. Few of us have any use for this principle today, whatever its merits. We may, however, hotly dispute a principle which demands that one always answer the telephone, even if it encroaches on well-deserved and desperately needed privacy.

Ironically enough, both he who is so rigidly principled that he can no longer flexibly deal with the problems of everyday life and he who is so lethargically passive that every impulse drives him in another direction miss what it means for man to be alive.

The tension in human existence that man must creatively employ persists between values and meaning. A value suggests that a certain person, object, or event is more important or precious than another. We must be willing to sacrifice the less-valued object in our possession for the higher-valued one we want to gain. In biblical language: A man must be willing to sell all he has in order to buy the one precious pearl. Or someone may forgo the pleasure of a trip in order to buy an expensive fur coat or racing car. Values impress on man the need actively and decisively to choose.

Meaning, on the contrary, is discovered when we dare to cease active selecting. With a reflective distance from immediate involvement we begin to ask ourselves why we are so eagerly seeking to better our life. The tension between values and meaning represents the stark difference between an attitude of reflective meditation and active pursuit without reflection. The Eastern mood of quiet reflection is best expressed in the biblical question what man would gain if he won the whole world but lost his soul in the process. The Western incentive for unflagging work and achievement inspired the prayer of St. Ignatius Loyola: "Teach us, good Lord, to serve Thee as Thou deservest: To give and not to count the cost; to fight and not to heed the wounds; to toil and not to seek for rest; to labour and not ask for any reward save that of knowing that we do Thy will."

Clearly, absolute passivity is as little a viable option as is senseless activism. Man must keep in fragile balance the suggestiveness of values and the overall sense of direction that expresses meaning. Translated into sexual concern, this means that the constant lure of new and more exciting pleasure must be kept in balance with the ever present reminder that true enjoyment and pleasure do not necessarily arise from a new object but may come from a fresh attitude on our part. Stimulus and response must equal each other if sex is to be the experience of a mutually creative exchange.

The death of love occurs when man retreats into the cave of

sullen isolation from the honest exchange of interpersonal worth. If we dare to stand the threat of naked encounter we may discover that the fundamental meaning of life lies in living freely and creatively together. Dynamic, self-expressive life, which is how love is best defined, creates its own meaning. All that persons can do is make sense.

The meaning of man's life is love. Values, however, introduce always a separatist note and thereby endanger the corporate love life. Meaning unites and re-creates people. He who before understood himself on his own premises, discovers now that the meaning of his life is to express through living the corporate nature of human existence. Values suggest comparison and competition. Do I value my spouse enough? Or could I have married a partner with different qualities? Does my partner recognize me for what I really am? Or will I find myself suddenly replaced by a competitor who has more to give? Values not firmly rooted in the supreme meaning of a corporate life act as tempting, seductive lure, breaking the common life in favor of a selfish quest for one's own gain.

The tension between values and meaning is a seeming paradox which, nevertheless, comprises the very incentive for human living. Discovery and experience provide the essential flow in man's life. Man is neither a precious island to himself, cherishing nothing so highly as his individual privacy, nor an irrelevant, invalid particle in a meaningless mass. He is a corporate being. His personal growth is inseparably involved with the whole development of mankind. Neither is possible without the other.

We cannot always scrutinize beforehand the unconscious depth out of which our profound drives and motivations arise. Nor can we always maintain with equal clarity the far-reaching vision of what renders existence meaningful. But we can develop a critical eye for those values which attract and animate us. We can ask in honest conversation whether our desires and goals improve our living together or promote estrangement from each other. We can value our common life higher than individual pleasure. We can decide either to forgo what we seek for ourselves or to sacrifice our living together. This decision must be faced on its own merits. No moral, religious, or social principle can decide whether two partners can truly grow together or must separate for the sake of their individual growth. In these decisions we try to make sense. We link what emerges out of fantasy through imagination with reflection on the purposeful development of our life. We aim at more confident self-awareness as we experience with passionate immediacy and reflect with serene detachment. We gain insight and guidance while we live on the hope that there is some meaning in our being alive and living together.

# CONCLUSION

THE AMERICAN PEOPLE, as adolescents, in marriage, or as parents, are beginning to recognize that they shoulder the full responsibility for their lives without much dependable help from traditional authorities. Having achieved a broadly affluent society, our nation now faces the question: Can we make sense of what we have and produce? This question cannot be answered by a generalized government plan or a superimposed ideology. The people themselves must mature in order to shape in freedom a way of living together which renders their vast possessions and opportunities meaningful. Incorporating sex suggests one key to responding to the challenge of the day.

It has been argued here that sex loses its meaning when restricted to a prepared niche in life. Our being and acting as sexual creatures provide us with the challenge and opportunity to integrate the whole personality. Sex poses a dual task. At once highly personal and essentially interpersonal, sex indicates that neither escapist individualism nor mass anonymity can help us. As individuals we must fully participate in and contribute to the shaping of our society so that living together affords both a sense of independence and a freedom for involvement. Without independence we cannot play our social part. Without involvement we cannot achieve results.

In incorporating sex we can gain much by adopting the spirit and attitude that have carried the sciences to their present height. The scientific mood can free us to reconsider critically the traditional ways and means of controlling sex life. A scientific spirit would elicit willingness to experiment with new and better ways of living together as sexual beings.

A cautious reader may protest against such an approach because he believes sex to be far too explosive a force for us to experiment freely with its expressions. In fact, however, people are already experimenting in the area of sex. Although not officially sanctioned, premarital and extramarital sex are practiced as alternatives to the equation of sex and marriage. In spite of religious qualms and social disapproval, divorce and remarriage are common occurrences in our communities. The question thus is not whether to experiment, but how honest, clear-sighted, and creative we can be in our experimenting. As long as we soft-pedal the evidence of a sexual crisis and ignore the need for a better understanding of sex, we force people to depend on their limited insights.

The task of searching for a more realistic, confident attitude toward sex would be much easier if we could be scientific to the extent of relying exclusively on objective data. But sex is not merely a thing or circumstance. It involves human self-understanding and often dimly appreciated emotions. In method, therefore, we must go beyond scientific empiricism. No generalized, iron-clad prescription is possible for how any individual could or should go about incorporating sex.

Moreover, a reader may conclude that what is suggested here cannot be applied to his specific life situation. One or both partners in a sex relationship may not feel that they have the inner resources or inclination to embark on a mutual journey toward greater self-awareness and a more conscious incorporation of sex life. At least, this book has helped such a reader to arrive at that conclusion. Not to obey blindly or to reject outright, but to argue with and to amend his contentions will fulfill the author's intention.

The questions, pointers, and criteria offered here are meant for those people, young and old, who, for their own sake or because of their children, find themselves already forced to question and re-evaluate traditional ways of coping with sex. They are in a good position to weigh what has been proposed. Having read these pages they can undertake now their own verification of how much they have been helped.

The reader's attitude to this book should be scientific inasmuch as he is invited to treat it as an expanded hypothesis. It is up to him to test it in his own thought and experience. Each person, each couple must learn on their own how to live. Someone else's reflection can only prompt them to think about life more clearly and to maintain such a learning process with resolute vigor. Indifference to how we live and apathy toward a possible improvement of our way of life are no doubt the most dehumanizing forces in our society. No one is merely the downtrodden slave, nor is anyone the freelance master of personal destiny. Fate is forged both by how we understand as well as accept a given situation and how we respond imaginatively to the possibilities it still offers.

We must begin with ourselves, regardless of how difficult such a beginning at first appears. If we wait until circumstances change, we are bound to lose even more of our self-confidence. The conviction of this book is that the American people, especially the young, already have begun as persons to come into their own. However insecure and groping the beginning, it holds much promise and must be encouraged.